"This is an indispensable book for anyone interested in contemporary psychoanalytic theory and practice. In a definitive, highly original, and practically useful way, Dr. Katz augments and enriches our understanding of the concept of enactment by demonstrating that it is an ongoing unconscious process that plays a central role in every treatment. In doing so, he has made a major contribution to our field."

– Theodore J. Jacobs, MD,
Training and Supervising Analyst,
New York Psychoanalytic Institute and the
Institute for Psychoanalytic Education

"In *The Play Within the Play: The Enacted Dimension of Psychoanalytic Process,* Gil Katz gives us a much needed overview of thinking about enactments in clinical work. From a contemporary Freudian object relations perspective, he offers a comprehensive, fair-minded study of contributions from a wide range of theoretical traditions. Katz's book is a sure-handed guide through the complexities of this topic. Candidates and practitioners alike will be challenged to test their own thinking against his original observations and formulations."

– Jay Greenberg, PhD,
Training and Supervising Analyst,
William Alanson White Institute, and Editor,
The Psychoanalytic Quarterly

"This innovative book illustrates the extent to which psychoanalysis has truly evolved. Along with dreams, transference, and countertransference, contemporary analysts now consider enactment and nonverbal communication within the analytic dyad to be one of the main elements of clinical experience. This wonderful and original book by Gil Katz explores, expands, and creatively illustrates the 'enacted dimension of analytic process,' an unconscious transference–countertransference dimension of all treatments, in which unrepresented and pre-represented early experience finds expression and becomes available for analytic work. This rich and original contribution deepens our understanding of analytic process, and advances psychoanalytic theory and practice."

– Stefano Bolognini, MD,
President-Elect,
International Psychoanalytic Association

"Enactment is one of the many concepts in psychoanalysis that seems to become less clear the more it's used. In this volume Gil Katz bravely takes on this term, and explores it in depth, both theoretically and clinically.

D0165757

His exploration of this topic over the last 15 years led to his felicitous phrase 'the enacted dimension of analytic process,' capturing how ubiquitous and continuous it is within analytic process. His contemporary Freudian, object relations viewpoint brings fresh insights to our methods of understanding and working in this important arena of the psychoanalytic relationship."

– **Fred Busch**, PhD,
Training and Supervising Analyst,
PINE Psychoanalytic Center, and Faculty,
Boston Psychoanalytic Institute

THE PLAY WITHIN THE PLAY
The Enacted Dimension of Psychoanalytic Process

In *The Play Within the Play: The Enacted Dimension of Psychoanalytic Process*, Gil Katz presents and illustrates the "enacted dimension of psychoanalytic process." He clarifies that enactment is not simply an overt event but an unconscious, continuously evolving, dynamically meaningful process.

Using clinical examples, including several extended case reports, Gil Katz demonstrates how in all treatments, a new version of the patient's early conflicts, traumas, and formative object relationships is inevitably created, without awareness or intent, in the here-and-now of the analytic dyad. Within the enacted dimension, repressed or dissociated aspects of the patient's past are not just remembered, they are relived. Katz shows how, when the enacted dimension becomes conscious, it forms the basis for genuine and transforming experiential insight.

Gil Katz is a Clinical Associate Professor of Psychology, Faculty Member, and Supervising Analyst at the NYU Postdoctoral Program in Psychotherapy and Psychoanalysis, where he also chairs the Faculty and Curriculum Committee of the Contemporary Freudian Track. He is a Faculty Member and Fellow (Training and Supervising Analyst) at the Institute for Psychoanalytic Training and Research (IPTAR), where he has also served as Dean of Training. Dr. Katz teaches courses on enacted processes in psychoanalytic treatment at both institutes.

RELATIONAL PERSPECTIVES BOOK SERIES
LEWIS ARON & ADRIENNE HARRIS
Series Editors

RELATIONAL PERSPECTIVES BOOK SERIES
LEWIS ARON & ADRIENNE HARRIS
Series Editors

RELATIONAL PERSPECTIVES BOOK SERIES

LEWIS ARON & ADRIENNE HARRIS
Series Editors

RELATIONAL PERSPECTIVES BOOK SERIES
LEWIS ARON & ADRIENNE HARRIS
Series Editors

THE PLAY WITHIN THE PLAY

The Enacted Dimension of Psychoanalytic Process

Gil Katz

Routledge
Taylor & Francis Group

LONDON AND NEW YORK

First published 2014
by Routledge
27 Church Road, Hove, East Sussex BN3 2FA

Simultaneously published in the USA and Canada
by Routledge
711 Third Avenue, New York, NY 10017

Routledge is an imprint of the Taylor & Francis Group, an informa business

British Library Cataloguing in Publication Data
A catalogue record for this book is available from the British
Library

Library of Congress Cataloging in Publication Data
Katz, Gil A.
The play within the play : the enacted dimension of
psychoanalytic process / Gil A. Katz.
pages cm.—
(Relational perspectives book series ; 56)
1. Psychoanalysis.   2. Acting out (Psychology)   I. Title.
BF173.K3698 2013
616.89'17—dc23
2013006553

ISBN: 978-0-415-81966-4 (hbk)
ISBN: 978-0-415-81967-1 (pbk)
ISBN: 978-0-203-79892-8 (ebk)

Typeset in Garamond
by RefineCatch Limited, Bungay, Suffolk, UK

SUSTAINABLE
FORESTRY
INITIATIVE

Certified Sourcing
www.sfiprogram.org
SFI-00555
The SFI label applies to the text stock.

Printed and bound in the United States of America by
Walsworth Publishing Company, Marceline, MO.

FOR MARY AND RACHEL

CONTENTS

CONTENTS

ACKNOWLEDGMENTS

I am indebted to my students at NYU Postdoc and IPTAR who, over the years, have helped me clarify concepts and taught me a great deal about the enacted dimension of analytic process. The candidates at both of these institutes have a wonderful curiosity and openness to the growth and change that has characterized psychoanalytic theory and practice over the past 30 years.

I am also indebted to Norbert Freedman who died this past year. Bert was a generative teacher, an energetic leader, and a loving friend. I had known Bert for almost 40 years. He hired me for my first job after graduate school at Downstate Medical Center, and I worked with him there for two decades. He was an influential teacher during my training at NYU Postdoc in the late 1970s and early 1980s, and then we were colleagues for almost 20 years at Postdoc and at IPTAR. His influence on me, on the development of several generations of psychoanalysts, and on the evolution of contemporary Freudian psychoanalysis in New York City, is immeasurable. His presence continues to be felt, and missed, in the many professional arenas in which he was so central.

Thanks to Lew Aron, co-editor of this book series, for his encouragement and assistance throughout every phase of this book. It was a special pleasure discussing and debating ideas with him. Thanks also to my other co-editor, Adrienne Harris, for her thoughtful input and for helping pave the way to the book's publication.

My deep gratitude to the colleagues who carefully read and generously commented on earlier drafts of this book: many thanks to Andrew Druck, Margery Kalb, Richard Lasky, and Bruce Reis for their invaluable feedback, suggestions, and support. I also want to thank Margery for introducing me to the work of Stefano Bolognini. Special thanks to the members of my peer group, Judith Hanlon, Mary Libbey, and Seymour Moscovitz, who reviewed several drafts of the book as it progressed. We have been meeting regularly for over 30 years. Judy, Mary, and Seymour have been a central part of all my intellectual endeavors and professional growth and have become deep friends. Most of all, I thank my wife Mary and my daughter Rachel for their love, encouragement, and unfailing support throughout this project.

The image on the book jacket – a depiction of the "play within the play" scene from *Hamlet*, Act III, Scene 2 – is a photograph of a wood jigsaw puzzle that was made between 1910 and 1920 in London, England. It is part of a collection of old jigsaw puzzles which can be found on the website "Bob Armstrong's Old Puzzles" www.oldpuzzles.com. When I came across this photo I was taken not only by its subject matter, but also by the aptness of its being a jigsaw puzzle. Both features together seemed a delightful metaphor for the puzzle that unfolds and is put together in a psychoanalytic treatment, and how the play within the play is a significant piece of that puzzle. I am indebted to Bob Armstrong, owner of the website, for his kind permission to use the image for the book.

Portions of this book are based on or excerpted from earlier works that I published. Material from my 1988 paper "Where the action is: The enacted dimension of analytic process," *Journal of the American Psychoanalytic Association, 46*, 1129–1167 forms the basis of much of Part I of this book, and portions of Part II. With permission from Sage Publications, which holds the copyright, this material has been rewritten and reworked for this book.

The extensive excerpts in Chapter 6 from Patrick Casement's case of Mrs. B are taken from his 1982 paper, "Some pressures on the analyst for physical contact during the re-living of an early trauma," *International Review of Psycho-Analysis, 9*, 279–86, with permission from Wiley Press. My thanks to Patrick Casement for his comments on this chapter.

The case presentation and discussion in Chapter 9 were originally presented at an inter-orientation colloquium on enactment sponsored by the Contemporary Freudian track of the NYU Postdoctoral Program in Psychotherapy and Psychoanalysis that took place in March 2009. Anthony Bass and I discussed Katherine Oram's case, and Desnee Hall chaired the meeting. I am grateful to Katherine Oram and her patient for their permission to use their clinical material.

Chapter 10 is an adaptation of my discussion of Dale Boesky's "Parallel process and supervision," presented at a Scientific Meeting, chaired by Phyllis Beren, of the Institute for Psychoanalytic Training and Research (IPTAR) in March 2005. Many thanks to Dale Boesky and Jean-Paul Pegeron for their comments on this chapter. Pegeron's supervisory vignette, which also appeared in his 1996 paper, "Supervision as an analytic experience," *Psychoanalytic Quarterly, 65*, 693–710, is reproduced in its entirety with permission from the *Psychoanalytic Quarterly* who holds the copyright.

Chapter 11 is an adaptation of a panel discussion, chaired by Jay Frankel, which took place at a meeting of the Investigative Section of the Institute for Psychoanalytic Training and Research (IPTAR) in January 2007 entitled, "Perspectives on dissociation." The paper presentations by Wilma Bucci and Siri Erika Gullestad, and my formal discussion of these papers, have been extensively reworked for this book. My thanks to Wilma Bucci and Siri Gullestad for their contributions to this panel and to this chapter of the book. Gullestad's clinical vignette, the case of Sara, is reproduced in its entirety from her 2005 paper, "Who is 'who' in dissociation? A plea for psychodynamics in a time of trauma," *International Journal of Psycho-analysis*, 86, 639–56, with permission from Wiley Press.

Chapter 12 was first published as "Missing in action: The enacted dimension of analytic process in a patient with traumatic object loss," in Richard Lasky (Ed.), *Symbolization and desymbolization: Essays in honor of Norbert Freedman* (pp. 407–430), New York: Other Press, 2002. It is reprinted here, with minor revisions, with permission of Other Press.

The material in Chapter 13 was originally published in Andrew B. Druck, Carolyn Ellman, Norbert Freedman, and Aaron Thaler (Eds.), *A new Freudian synthesis: Clinical process in the next generation* (pp. 219–247), London: Karnac Books, 2011. The clinical case was originally titled: "Secretly attached, secretly separate: Art, dreams, and transference–countertransference in the analysis of a third generation Holocaust survivor"; the discussion of the case was originally titled: "Trauma in action: The enacted dimension of analytic process in a third generation Holocaust survivor." They are reprinted here, with some minor reworking, with kind permission of Karnac Books. I am grateful to Michal Talby-Abarbanel and her patient for their permission to use her paper.

INTRODUCTION

I became interested in the topic of enactment after I was asked to teach a course on the subject at the NYU Postdoctoral Program in 1996. The course was entitled, "Interaction in Psychoanalysis: Transference, Counter-transference, and Enactment" – and with what I learned preparing that course, and with what my students in that first class helped me clarify, I wrote the 1998 paper, "Where the action is: The enacted dimension of analytic process." In truth, I have always been interested in unconscious communication and the nonverbal aspects of the treatment process (having always been more of a nonverbal kind of person myself), and I had previously written on such topics as the use of metaphor in analytic treatment, and the parallel process phenomenon in analytic supervision (a version of which constitutes Chapter 10).

The treatment process I wrote about in the 2002 paper, "Missing in action: The enacted dimension of analytic process in the treatment of a patient with traumatic object loss" (reprinted in Chapter 12) was actually conducted in the mid-1980s, before the concept of enactment (Jacobs, 1986; Johan, 1992) came into being. Back then, I conceptualized what occurred in the treatment in terms of the concepts of the day, such as projective identification and concordant and complementary countertransference, and presented the case at the 1993 Division 39 meeting with the title "A death in the countertransference." Then, after writing the 1998 paper, I returned to the case and reconceptualized my understanding of it in terms of enactment.

As further background, I would also like to say something about the major influences on my analytic thinking and development. The cumulative writings of Hans Loewald, with his object relations conceptualization of Freudian theory and his developmental perspective on clinical work, shaped my early overall approach to psychoanalysis, and the contemporary writings of Ted Jacobs have been specifically instrumental in shaping my ideas on enactment and the realm of unconscious and nonverbal communication in psychoanalytic work. Today, I would describe myself as a contemporary Freudian who emphasizes the unconscious interpenetration of transference–countertransference dynamics – what I will be calling the *interpsychic* level of analytic process – as they evolve within the analytic relationship, as an important route to understanding the patient. Perhaps "Object-Relational Freudian" is the most apt designation. The differences between this orientation and a relational orientation will I hope become evident over the course of this book.

I introduced the concept of the "enacted *dimension* of analytic process" 15 years ago (1998, 2002) because I was not happy with the term "enactment," nor with most of the existing definitions at the time. The word "enactment" itself suggests an episodic or discrete event, and discussions in the literature tended to emphasize the behavioral component of the phenomenon. To my mind, however, the essence of what needed to be conceptualized was a dynamically evolving, unconscious process. As I hope this book will illustrate, enactments are not exceptional occurrences; they are, rather, the continuous background of the work of analysis. Enactments are actually transference and countertransference using an alternate channel to gain expression. Rather than being expressed via the verbally symbolic channel – through thoughts, feelings, and fantasies – they are expressed via the action channel, which includes not only motor behavior, but also silence, and even speech itself. Analytic process thus comprises two dimensions that are continuously interwoven: the familiar verbally symbolized dimension (free-association, interpretation, etc.), and the enactively symbolized dimension in which unconscious, nonverbal communications between patient and analyst are continuously taking place.

The book is an effort to clarify the conceptual issues related to enactment and the enacted dimension rather than a systematic comparison of psychoanalytic schools. It is divided into four parts. In Part I, I take up the evolutionary changes in psychoanalytic theory that led to the concept of enactment. Chapter 1 reviews the historical confusion around the role of action and repetition in psychoanalytic theory and practice and how the reconceptualization of action has led to a fuller understanding of the concepts of transference and countertransference, one that includes the enacted dimension of each. Chapter 2 considers transference and countertransference as a unit – the transference–countertransference matrix – and presents early conceptualizations of the enacted dimension of analytic process: projective identification, role-responsiveness, countertransference structures, unconsciously negotiated resistance, and transformation and resisting transformation. Chapter 3 discusses the emergence of the term *enactment,* its widespread acceptance as an important psychoanalytic concept as well as the lack of consensus, and the ongoing confusion, over its definition.

Part II presents the concept of the *enacted dimension of analytic process.* Chapter 4 outlines the concept of the dual dimensionality of analytic process, along with its neurobiological correlates suggested by research being conducted in the field of cognitive neuroscience, and Chapter 5 illustrates the continuous presence and centrality of the enacted dimension through two vignettes from the literature, one by Joseph Sandler and the other by Owen Renik. Chapter 6 reconsiders another treatment from the literature, this one by Patrick Casement that he discussed in two separate papers, that illustrates two levels of preverbal experience that had been relived in the enacted dimension. Chapter 7 develops the concept of *interpsychic* interaction – the unconscious and preconscious transference–countertransference processes that underlie the enacted dimension of analytic process – and differentiates it from *interpersonal* interaction, *intersubjectivity,* and the *analytic third.* It also addresses the contemporary concept of *co-creation* or *co-construction.* Does characterizing an enactment as "co-created" clarify or obscure the nature of the dynamic process involved? What exactly is it that is co-created? Chapter 8 concerns the relationship between enactment and analytic technique. Does our understanding of enacted transference–countertransference processes affect how we conduct analytic treatment? Do we need to alter our technical principles? Have they even, as some have suggested, become obsolete and expendable? Chapter 9 presents a 13-year treatment of a man with lifelong sexual inhibitions and illustrates how overt behavioral "enactments" around session frequency, hand-holding, and countertransference expressions of anger are more usefully understood as actualizations of important developmental events and internalized object relationships being reexperienced in the enacted dimension of the treatment. Chapter 10 considers the enacted dimension of analytic supervision, what has previously been called the parallel process phenomenon.

Part III offers three extended clinical reports illustrating the centrality of the enacted dimension in the treatment of patients who have endured various forms of severe trauma. Chapter 11 presents the treatment of a woman with Dissociated Identity Disorder who suffered extreme sexual abuse as a child. It considers both neurobiological and psychodynamic formulations of the patient's dissociative processes and illustrates the enacted dimension of the treatment process. Chapter 12 is the treatment case I published in 2002 that illustrates how a patient's dissociated object loss was relived, with the unconscious participation of the analyst, in the enacted dimension thereby becoming available for mourning and reparative analytic work. Chapter 13, a supervised case, illustrates how the wordless and unverbalizable sequella of the Holocaust trauma was unconsciously transmitted across three generations and became the essential feature of the enacted dimension of the treatment of a third-generation survivor.

The final part of the book presents the frequent and common questions I am asked when I have presented these ideas in various psychoanalytic forums. I hope the answers provided here will address at least some of the questions that arise in your mind as you read this book.

Part I

THEORETICAL EVOLUTION

The core concepts of psychoanalysis have undergone substantial evolution over the past century. Changes in our understanding of the role of action transformed our conception of transference and countertransference and expanded our understanding of the ways in which early experience finds expression in treatment. Additionally, every analytic school has now integrated the interactional aspects of the analytic relationship into its theory of mind. Out of these developments, the concept of enactment emerged to describe a central feature of the transference–countertransference matrix, one that has enhanced our understanding of clinical process and the therapeutic action of psychoanalysis.

1

IN THE BEGINNING

The Talking Cure and the Problem of Action

The concepts of transference, acting out, and repetition were introduced together, early in Freud's writing (1905, 1912a, 1914). Despite their intertwined beginnings, psychoanalytic thinking about transference and action developed along separate paths, the latter in both neglected and disfavored fashion. In his review of action and acting out, Roughton (1996, p. 130) notes that "from the very beginning of 'the talking cure,' there has been a strong tendency to exclude action, both in fact and in theory, from this mostly verbal process."

Yet Freud linked the two concepts. He viewed transference both as a way of remembering and as a resistance to remembering (1912a). And he viewed acting out not only as a resistance to remembering, but also as a way of remembering (1914, p. 150, emphases in the original):

> The patient does not *remember* anything of what he has forgotten and repressed, but *acts* it out. He reproduces it not as a memory but as an action; he *repeats* it, without, of course, knowing that he is repeating it. . . . As long as he is in the treatment he cannot escape from this compulsion to repeat; and in the end we understand that this is his way of remembering.

For Freud, acting out was a clinical concept directly related to transference: acting out was *always* transference, and the entire transference was an acting out, one that was essential for the treatment – as he noted, "One cannot overcome an enemy who is absent or not within range" (1914, p. 152). "We must treat the patient's illness," he said, "not as an event of the past, but as a present day force" (Freud, 1914, p. 150). Consider Freud's three examples of acting out:

> The patient does not say that he remembers that he used to be defiant and critical towards his parents' authority; instead, he behaves that way toward the doctor. He does not remember how

3

he came to a helpless and hopeless deadlock in his infantile sexual researches; but he produces a mass of confused dreams and associations, complains that he cannot succeed in anything and asserts that he is fated never to carry through what he undertakes. He does not remember having been intensely ashamed of certain sexual activities and afraid of their being found out; but he makes it clear that he is ashamed of the treatment on which he is now embarked and tries to keep it secret from everybody.

(Freud, 1914, p. 150)

Not only is there no behavioral action in these examples, today we would consider them to be simply transference rather than acting out. Clearly, Freud did not sharply differentiate the two concepts. Both could constitute a resistance at one point and an indispensable tool for analytic work at another. Both seemed to be part of a conceptually broader category of repetition, but Freud did not make it clear how they differed from each other in this regard.

In discussing acting out in his later writings, Freud (1940, p. 177) also expressed concern that a patient's actions outside the treatment setting could seriously interfere with the treatment and suggested that "the ideal conduct for our purposes would be that he should behave as normally as possible outside the treatment and express his abnormal reactions only in the transference." Analysts since Freud, overemphasizing this statement, have generally defined acting out as *motor* behavior, primarily *outside* the treatment setting, that served as a *resistance* to analysis (for thorough reviews of the concept of acting out, see Abend, 1993; Boesky, 1982; Kanzer, 1966; Roughton, 1996). Less attention was paid to Freud's statements linking acting out with transference in which he described forms of action *within* the analytic setting which, like free association, could also serve a *communicative* function.

The last two decades of the twentieth century saw a reversal of this trend, resulting in two major changes in the concept of acting out and the role of action. The first, a correction of the historical overemphasis on resistance, is by now well established and widely accepted: action – in or out of the treatment, behavioral or verbal – is no longer seen simply as a discharge product opposed to transference and impeding the treatment. It is now understood as a product of the mind, the equivalent of other forms of unconscious communication and resistance. Ekstein's admonition over 45 years ago is now a commonplace: "as we are impartial toward the *content* [of the patient's communication] we must also learn to be impartial toward the *mode of communication*" (1965, p. 171, emphases in the original).

The second major change is a correction of the overemphasis on *motor* action. Contemporary psychoanalytic interest has shifted away from the

4

mostly external motor actions generally referred to by the term acting out, and is now attending to more subtle forms of action occurring *within* the analytic dyad. Concepts like "enactment," "actualization," "reliving," and "living out in the transference" have all but replaced "acting out" in psychoanalytic discourse. Not only do these newer concepts place less emphasis on motor behavior; they also return to Freud's point that acting out and transference are two forms of remembering and repeating, two vehicles for the expression of the patient's psychic reality.

Thus, the aforementioned contemporary terms represent the conceptual reuniting of Freud's intertwined concepts, acting out and transference. They recognize that transference (as well as countertransference, as I will discuss shortly) may be represented not only through verbal symbols but also through *enacted processes* – unconscious psychic processes that use behavior, silence, and even speech as symbolic vehicles. There is now general consensus that enacted manifestations of transference are integral accompaniments of the verbally symbolized transference and are intrinsic to analytic process and the therapeutic action of psychoanalysis.

The Enacted Dimension of Transference

The last three decades of the twentieth century saw many analytic writers expand our understanding of transference to include its enacted dimension. One of the earliest and most influential contributors to this subject was Hans Loewald (1960, 1970, 1971, 1975, 1976), who legitimized and ultimately elevated its role. Loewald made the clarification that Freud's contrasting of remembering and repeating was meant to elucidate two different modes of psychic functioning, but not to imply that they were mutually exclusive. In Loewald's view, the conscious mental act of remembering – what he called "representational memory" – is a kind of repetition that occurs in the psychical field, and repeating in the form of action – what he called "enactive memory" – is an unconscious form of remembering. Thus, within the analytic setting, action, as an unconscious memorial activity, is a vehicle of communication and a useful form of transference.

Boesky (1982) argued for the formal integration of Freud's concept of acting out with the related concepts of transference, repetition, and working through. In his definition of acting out, Boesky emphasized the centrality of unconscious fantasy and compromise formation. He considered acting out to contain two components: an unconscious transference fantasy and a concomitant action or behavior. Building on discussions of "actualization" by Laplanche and Pontalis (1967) and Sandler (1976), Boesky maintained that when the ego experiences the imminent futility, or danger, of an unconscious fantasy's becoming actualized in the transference, action can facilitate a compromise formation that simultaneously carries out the wish and defends against it: "what becomes relevant ... is the fate of the unconscious transference fantasy and its tendency toward actualization rather than the coincidental motor action or behavior which might or might not accompany it as an aspect of the compromise formation engendered by the fantasy" (1982, p. 46).

To emphasize its status as a legitimate product of the mind, Boesky usefully compared acting out to dreams:[1] the day residue that prompts dreams corresponds to the transference residue that prompts acting out; the complexity of condensations in dreams corresponds to the complexity of compromise formations in acting out; the hallucinatory reality of dreams corresponds to the false reality created by acting out; the manifest content and the latent content of dreams correspond to the two components of acting out – the action itself and the underlying transference fantasy; the secondary revision of dreams corresponds to the patient's rationalizations about acting out; and both phenomena contain an adaptive potential – active, nonregressive components that are related to the process of working through.

Boesky summed up the centrality of action and "acting out" in psychoanalytic treatment as follows: "Psychoanalysis can not take place without acting out any more than psychoanalysis could take place without transference. Acting out is the potential of the transference neurosis for actualization and therefore expresses the psychic reality of the transference" (1982, p. 52). Thus, Boesky firmly linked acting out with transference. Steingart (1995, p. 135) considered most acting out to *be* transference – a transference organization that "incorporates an urge for action of one sort or another in the psychoanalytic relationship." In the terms I am developing here, Freud's original concept of acting out would refer to the *enacted dimension of transference*.

While many have called for a general psychoanalytic theory of action (Boesky, 1982; Hartmann, 1964; Rangell, 1989), the conceptualization of action as a dimension of transference places action in a different light. As Roughton (1996) suggests, action per se is not in fact a psychoanalytically meaningful term, since action is ubiquitous in the clinical process and encompasses all motivated behavior from thinking, feeling, remembering, and talking at one end, to observable motor behavior at the other: "Action, thus broadly defined, by itself has no clinical psychoanalytic significance, just as the chemistry of an artist's paints is vital to his or her work but has nothing to do with the choice of subject or the experience of the viewer" (Roughton, 1996, p. 141). In Roughton's view, the psychoanalytically meaningful questions about action in the clinical setting are about *which* actions are carried out and *why* – that is, they concern motivation, conflict, and psychic functioning.

I would add, and will address in the remainder of this book, that the relevant questions about action also concern the very nature of transference – the nature of both its enacted and its verbally symbolized dimensions. For instance, what do enacted transference processes tell us about the nature of the patient's experience of the treatment? What do they tell us about early traumatic experiences? What do they tell us about the quality of the patient's psychological orientation to reality, or the level of his or her ego development? Is transference expression in the enacted sphere inevitable, and are shifts between the two spheres an essential part of working through, as Freud suggested?

Both Busch (1989, 1995) and Loewald (1975) added a developmental perspective to these issues, further explicating the nature of the enacted dimension of transference. In discussing forms of transference in which words and language are not used symbolically but rather are used as actions, Busch points out that while psychoanalysis considers the verbal period to begin at about 18 months, words and thought are actually under the domination of action for a much longer period. Speech may thus constitute action that symbolizes something in addition to, or even entirely different from, its verbal content. Busch's concept of "action-thoughts" and Loewald's concept of "language action" (see also Levenson's [1983] use of the term "language act") designate forms of verbal repetition in action that originate in the early pre-operational, concrete-operations stage of thinking (ages two to five), when talk and action are not yet fully distinguished. During this stage the child is in the process of transforming the earlier action mode of thinking into a new arena, the mental, in which reality can be represented internally.[2] Mental experience in this stage, however, continues to remain closer to overt action. Since the psychic conflicts and traumas that create adult psychopathology are formed during this stage, the central role of repression and dissociation insures that action-thinking and language action will continue into adulthood outside the patient's awareness. Thus, in Busch's view, the compulsion to repeat in action may be seen as a natural consequence of neurosis, and action-thoughts – "memories in action" – are viewed as an inevitable and necessary component of remembering (see also Reis's [2009] discussion of the role of enactive memory in the process of analytic witnessing). Interpreting action-thoughts allows experiences under the domination of pre-operational thought to be examined via higher-level thought processes.

Rather than saying, as I did above, that action-thoughts, or language action, are forms of transference in which words and language are not used symbolically but are used as actions, it is more accurate to say that such forms of transference represent early pre-stages of symbolization, or alternate channels of symbolization, that exist side by side, in an ongoing way, with reflective-verbal symbolization. Indeed, contemporary research in the fields of attachment theory, infant research, and cognitive neuroscience has demonstrated that sensorimotor and action-dominated modes of experiencing, thinking, remembering, and communicating are an intrinsic feature of human functioning at all stages of development. In analytic work, we now appreciate the extent to which such enactive, subsymbolic (Bucci, 1997), procedural (Clyman, 1991), and implicit (Lyons-Ruth, 1999) ways of encoding and remembering experience are a continuous aspect of the process. It is in this enacted dimension of the transference that early experience finds representation and expression in an affectively alive and immediate way. As Loewald (1975, pp. 293–94, emphasis in the original) describes:

> In the course of the psychoanalytic process, narrative is drawn into the context of transference dramatization, into the force-field of re-enactment. Whether in the form of free associations or more consciously, logically controlled trains of thought, narrative in psychoanalysis is increasingly being revealed in its character as language action, as symbolic action and in particular as language action within the transference force-field. The reference in regard to content and emotional tone of the communication through narrative, shifts more and more to their relevance as transference repetitions and transference actions in the psychoanalytic situation. One might express this by saying we take the patient less and less as speaking merely *about* himself, about his experiences and memories, and more and more as symbolizing action in speech, as speaking from the depth of his memories, which regain life and poignancy by the impetus and urgency of reexperience in the present of the analytic situation.

In the more reflective phases of treatment, "what was re-enactment, by reflection changes to that more objective repetition which Freud has called reproduction in the psychical field, as against reproduction by action" (1975, p. 296). Effective clinical practice, in Loewald's view, fosters an optimal balance and an ongoing interchange between what I am calling the enacted and the verbally symbolized dimensions of treatment. (See Singer & Conway, 2011; Vivona, 2003, 2006, 2009b for contemporary appreciations of Loewald's theories of the interplay between enactive and representational forms of language, experience, and memory, in both human development and therapeutic process.)

In Loewald's view, the core of the transference neurosis consists of experiences understood and resolved in an action form in the psychoanalytic situation.[3] Thus, Loewald views repetition in the form of re-enactment as the sine qua non of the transference neurosis. Analyzing this enacted dimension of transference, as I am calling it, provides depth of feeling, meaning, and understanding that is not present in analyzing thoughts alone. This is similar to Poland's view (1992b) that it is the actualization of the patient's past in the present interaction with the analyst – what he calls an "original creation" – that is the essential subject matter of effective analytic process.

The Enacted Dimension of Countertransference

Enacted processes are also a dimension of the analyst's *countertransference*. Like acting out, countertransference was at first viewed primarily as a resistance to analysis that the analyst needs to overcome (Freud, 1910, 1912b, 1915a). Conceptually linked to abstinence, countertransference, again like acting out, became excessively tied to overt behavior.[4] General acceptance of the broad, or "totalistic," conception of countertransference (Heimann, 1950; Racker, 1957), as opposed to the original "narrow" definition of countertransference (Reich, 1950), was instrumental in diminishing the exclusively negative/resistant connotation of countertransference and initiated a long-needed study of other facets of the analyst's subjective involvement in the clinical process.[5] However, as I will discuss in more depth in Chapter 3, it was not until the late 1980s and early 1990s, with the introduction of the contemporary Freudian concept of enactment and the advent of relational theories that emphasized the analyst's subjectivity, that the study of the analyst's unconscious contribution to the treatment process began in earnest. Regarding the place of enactment as an aspect of countertransference, it should be noted that neither the "narrow" definition of countertransference (*unconscious* aspects of the analyst's involvement that *interfere* with the analysis) nor the "totalistic" definition (which highlighted the *conscious* aspects of the analyst's experience that could be used to *further* the treatment), addressed the realm of unconscious enactment – aspects of the analyst's *unconscious* involvement in the analytic interaction that could also contribute *positively* to the therapeutic action of psychoanalysis.

In order to pull together the changes in the concepts of action, transference, and countertransference discussed thus far, I will present a brief vignette provided by Busch (1989, pp. 536–37).

> Mr. A was a "good patient" who had no difficulty supplying thoughts and feelings, and who generally responded to interpretation with confirmatory associations and memories. Nevertheless, little analytic progress was being made. Over time, the analyst realized that the content of the patient's words was not as important as the form they took: the patient was not really talking "to" the analyst, but talking "for" the analyst; he was not really "telling"

the analyst his thoughts, he was actually "giving" them to him. The patient's *verbal action* was the symbolic equivalent of his childhood actions designed to please his mother, who, during his toilet training begun at the age of one, waited with him in the bathroom until he had a bowel movement.

This vignette offers a good example, as Busch notes, of an enacted transference process in which words were used not as verbal symbols but as enacted symbols. If we focus, however, on the analyst's side of the couch, we might ask why this interaction went on for the length of time it did. Let us assume, hypothetically, that the patient's enacted transference gratified an unconsciously determined infantile need in the analyst to "get" from the patient "good" material that in turn contributed to the reported "transference resistance." Important to this discussion is that this hypothetical countertransference was not, initially, verbally symbolized in the analyst's mind but rather was enacted in the analytic interaction.

But more relevant to the central topic of this book, this unconscious analyst–patient fit, far from being disadvantageous for the treatment, unintentionally provided the patient with an analytic environment in which his infantile relationship with his mother was symbolically actualized – *remembered* in the enacted dimension of the treatment. For an unplanned and temporary period of time, it suffused the patient's infantile wishes and defenses toward his maternal object with an *analytic* reality, palpable and alive for both participants, in the "playground" of the transference (Freud, 1914, p. 154). The patient's transference became an "original creation" with his analyst, thereby enhancing its analyzability for both participants.

Thus, in addition to the *verbally symbolized* interaction between analyst and patient, the staple of the "talking cure" and traditionally considered the prime focus of analytic work, contemporary interest has now shifted to unconsciously *enacted* forms of interaction – unintended forms of transference–countertransference engage-ment in which the analyst's countertransference interpenetrates with, and actualizes, the patient's transference. This *enacted dimension of analytic process* occurs naturally and inevitably, without conscious awareness or intention. It exists alongside, and in concert with, the treatment's verbally symbolized content, an ongoing and evolving realm of analytic process with features unique to each analytic dyad. In these terms, the therapeutic action of psychoanalysis may be considered a function of two interwoven and inextricable treatment processes: transference experienced enactively and insight symbolized verbally.

As will be illustrated in the clinical examples presented in Parts II and III, even in what has traditionally been considered to be "standard" analytic treatment – treatment characterized by a reliance on verbally symbolized processes as the normative communicative mode and by a relative absence of gross behavioral action – an ongoing enacted *dimension,* more than we may have realized or acknowledged, regularly forms an integral part of the process.

Notes

1 A conceptualization of enactment as a two-party waking dream will be presented in Chapter 7.
2 During this earlier sensorimotor period, thought and action are identical and awareness is organized around sensorimotor schemata. Anthi (1983) and McLaughlin (1987) discuss such primitive enacted transferences in the clinical setting, and the possibilities of their being analyzed.
3 Freedman (1994) demonstrated how motor action in the clinical setting, rather than constituting the outcome of unsymbolizable conflict, may at times be a precursor to the transformation of psychic structure into higher levels of symbolization. As such, he too views the transference neurosis not as the reactivation of the infantile neurosis, but rather as the actualization of the unconscious fantasy in the here and now. This view is also central to Kern's (1987) conceptualization of the transference neurosis.
4 The recommendation that "the treatment must be carried out in abstinence" (1915, p.165) grew out of Freud's concerns about the experience of Breuer with Anna O., Jung with Sabina Spielrein, and himself with Dora.
5 For reviews of the historical evolution of the concept of countertransference, see Abend, 1989; Gabbard, 1995; Kernberg, 1965; Lasky, 1993.

2

FORERUNNERS

The Transference–Countertransference Matrix

There have been several important forerunners of the idea of an enacted dimension of analytic process. Prescient theorists from every corner of the psychoanalytic spectrum have foreshadowed today's interest in this unconscious, interactive dimension of analytic process. Dating back as early as the 1940s and 1950s, and writing from within such varied traditions as Kleinian, British object relations, Freudian, and Interpersonal, these theorists have proposed a variety of concepts that attempt to take formal theoretical account of the complex, unconscious interactions that evolve within the transference–countertransference matrix.[1]

In this chapter I will briefly summarize six conceptualizations of transference–countertransference interaction, each of which attempts to deal with one or more aspects of what I am calling the enacted dimension of clinical process: (1) the Kleinian concept of projective identification; (2) Joseph Sandler's concept of role-responsiveness; (3) Lucia Tower's concept of countertransference structures; (4) Hans Loewald's concept of a new object relationship; (5) Dale Boesky's concept of unconsciously negotiated resistance; and (6) Edgar Levenson's concept of transformation.

The next chapter will consider the advent of the contemporary Freudian concept of enactment and its wide acceptance and use by both Freudian and relational analysts. Differences between these two perspectives, revolving around the concepts of co-creation and analytic interaction, will be further elaborated in Part II.

Projective Identification

This term was coined by Melanie Klein (1946) to describe a primitive defense against paranoid/schizoid anxieties in which threatening parts of the ego are split off and projected into the object in an effort to rid the self of that which threatens to destroy it from within, and also to control and take possession of the object. Klein, however, addressed this process only as an intrapsychic fantasy in the patient. She did not address the patient's interactive process with the analyst, or any contribution the analyst might make to this process.

A dyadic, interactive dimension of this process was added by Bion (1959) who, using a developmental model, viewed the mother/analyst as the needed "container" of the primitive affective states that the child/patient could not yet regulate. The analyst, consciously or unconsciously, "contains" what the patient needs to project – holding it by temporarily deferring interpretation – until the patient is capable of experiencing it as part of the self.

Joseph (1989), focusing on the actual process of this analytic interaction, described the patient as attempting to unconsciously "nudge" the analyst into acting in a manner consistent with his or her projection, and the analyst as responding with internal, attenuated responses that can be used as data for interpretation. Joseph and other contemporary British Kleinians (see Schafer, 1997; Spillius, 1992) make substantial interpretive use of the analyst's psychic responses to the patient in the moment-to-moment flow of clinical process. However, Joseph stops short, as did Klein and Bion, of considering what contribution the analyst's own unconscious dynamics might make to the creation of this process, and so does not conceptualize the interactive process as unique to the particular patient–analyst dyad.

Role-Responsiveness

In contrast to these concepts of projective identification, Sandler's theoretical formulations take the step of including the analyst's unconscious dynamics in an interactive process unique to each analytic dyad. "Role-responsiveness" is part of Sandler's broad, object-relational consideration of transference–countertransference phenomena. Sandler (1976) considered transference to refer not only to the displacement of libidinal and aggressive wishes, but also to all the patient's attempts to manipulate or provoke situations with the analyst – through subtle verbal and non-verbal interactions – in order to *actualize,* within the framework and limits of the analytic situation, the intrapsychic self–object role relationship in which these unconscious wishes are embedded. This includes the role in which the patient casts him- or herself, and the complementary role in which he or she casts the analyst. Regarding countertransference, Sandler held that in addition to maintaining a "free-floating attention" to the patient, the analyst, within limits, responds to the patient with a "free-floating responsiveness" which includes not only thoughts and feelings, but attitudes and behavior. In Sandler's view, these responses, important elements in the analyst's "useful" countertransference, are compromise formations between the patient's pressure and the analyst's own unconscious tendencies.

Behavioral role-responsiveness thus entails the unintended, attenuated actualization of an unconscious wish, or defense against the wish, on the part of the analyst that may contribute to the patient's experience of transference actualization. The analyst may become aware of this participation only after it has been carried over into action, thus enabling the patient to remain unaware of the early internalized relationship he or she is trying to impose.

Sandler's concept of role-responsiveness overlaps with the Kleinian concept of projective identification, but differs from it in three critical ways.[2] First, it extends the idea of an interactive pull in the analytic relationship beyond the effects of a single primitive defensive maneuver on the part of the patient (projective identification) to the entire arena of multiply determined and layered transference phenomena from all levels of development and psychic organization. Second, it expands the concept of enacted psychic processes to include the *analyst's* unconscious processes. Third, behavioral role-responsiveness is seen as the product of a unique transference–countertransference fit that is an inevitable and unavoidable part of the treatment process.

Sandler does not, however, explore these interactive processes as an important *ongoing dimension* of analytic process, parallel to the verbally symbolized dimension, nor does he take up the question whether they are *integral* to the development and working through of the transference.

Countertransference Structures

While it predates Sandler's concept of behavioral role-responsiveness by 20 years, Tower's (1956) similar concept of "countertransference structures" goes further in the direction of my thesis.[3] Like role-responsiveness, a countertransference structure consists of the analyst's unconscious countertransference correspondence to the patient's particular transference – a unique pathological fit between transference and countertransference that is exploited by the unconscious pressure of the patient's transference:

> Every analyst of experience knows that as he gets deeper and deeper into an analysis, he somehow or other loses a certain perspective on the total situation. . . . it would appear that even under the most ideal circumstances there are bound to be certain drifts, so to speak, from the utterly straight direction of the analyst's performance and understanding of a case, and it is these very slow almost imperceptible drifts which develop in him in unconscious response to hidden pressures and motivations from his patient, which I think constitute the essence of the development of a countertransference structure in and of itself. . . . It is in the

nature of the transference resistances as they are built up by the patient that they should ferret out and hurl themselves against the weakest spots in the therapist's armamentarium.

(Tower, 1956, pp. 233–34)

Going further than Sandler, however, Tower viewed the development of a countertransference structure, whether a large or small part of the treatment as a whole, not only as inevitable and unavoidable, but also as an essential component of the curative process. As the counterpart of the transference neurosis, its understanding by the analyst is a necessary vehicle for the emotional understanding and final working through of the transference.

Perhaps the development of major change in the one, which is, after all, the purpose of the therapy, would be impossible without at least some minor change in the other, and it is probably relatively unimportant whether that minor change in the other is a rational one. It is probably far more important that the minor change in the other, namely, the therapist, be that which is specifically important and necessary to the one for whom we hope to achieve the major change. These changes in the therapist would be compounded in my view from the ego adaptive responses and the unconscious countertransferences of the analyst, interacting upon each other in such a way as to expand his ego integrative powers specifically to cope with the particular patient's transference resistances.

(Tower, 1956, p. 234)

Tower's lucid and remarkably prescient formulations of interactive enacted processes – her depiction of the existence of inevitable, naturally occurring enacted transference–countertransference processes that are unique to each analytic dyad and essential to the therapeutic action of psychoanalysis – comes closest to the thesis I am developing in this book. I will further suggest that these processes form an *ongoing dimension* – a second analytic text, if you will – that operates, without awareness, in concert with the verbally symbolized dimension of the treatment.

The New Object Relationship

The idea of an essential ongoing dimension of transference–countertransference process that remains largely unsymbolized on the verbal level is inherent in Loewald's (1960, 1979, 1986) concept of a "new object relationship." In Loewald's view (1986, p. 286), the patient's transference to the analyst is not only a repetition of old object

16

relationships, but also a new rendition that is "increasingly modified by the libidinally based transactions in the analytic encounter between patient and that special new object – the analyst." The ongoing juxtaposition, in the patient's experience, of both dimensions of transference provides him or her with the opportunity to reopen earlier lines of development within which new ways of relating to self and objects can be discovered.

Loewald (1986, p. 276) thus situates transference and countertransference in a developmental context in which they are viewed not as separate issues but as "two faces of the same dynamic, rooted in the inextricable intertwinings with others in which individual life originates, and remains throughout the life of the individual in numberless elaborations, derivatives, and transformations." One of these transformations, Loewald (1980, p. 376) observes, shows itself in the analytic encounter where, in deep unconscious layers, there coexist, along with more advanced levels of mental functioning and organization, "modes of *interpsychic* relatedness, of emotional ties that are active under the surface in both analysand and analyst, and thus in their relatedness, forming ingredients of the therapeutic potential" (emphasis added).

Additionally, Loewald (1986) placed emphasis on the analyst's emotional investment in the treatment process, acknowledged or not by patient or analyst. He proposed that this emotional investment – what he calls the "rapport facet" of the countertransference – is a decisive factor, though by no means the only one, in the curative process. He observes that "if the capacity for transference . . . is a measure of the patient's analyzability, the capacity for countertransference is a measure of the analyst's ability to analyze" (Loewald, 1986, pp. 285–86).

Loewald considered these features of the analytic relationship to be a nonexplicit background influence in all analytic treatment, a relatively constant factor in the treatment process. In this book I am highlighting an additional aspect of this ongoing analyst–patient interaction: unintended, enacted processes that result from the *unique* transference–countertransference fit of each analytic dyad.

Unconsciously Negotiated Resistance

Boesky's concept of "unconsciously negotiated resistance" brings the idea of inevitable, naturally occurring enacted transference–countertransference processes, unique to each analytic dyad and essential to the therapeutic action of psychoanalysis, within the framework of classical Freudian theory.

From what he called an *interactional perspective* within modern structural theory, Boesky (1990; in Hurst, 1995) expanded the concept of transference resistance to include an interactive form wherein the manifest shape taken by the resistance is unconsciously negotiated by both parties.[4] He considers the idea of a "pure" analytic treatment, in which all resistances are created only by the patient, to be a fiction.[5] As do Sandler and Tower, Boesky considers the analyst's contribution to these "usable" patterns of transference resistance to be a compromise formation, between the analyst's understanding the patient's and the analyst's own unconscious conflicts, which is used creatively without conscious awareness.

Emphasizing the uniqueness of each such transference–countertransference interaction, Boesky (1990) asserts that since the analyst's compromise formation would not have been necessary for another analyst, the resulting manifest form of the transference resistance is unique to the particular analytic dyad:

> the transference as *resistance* in any specific case is unique and would never, and could never, have developed in the identical manner, form, or sequence with any other analyst. *In fact, the manifest form of a resistance is even sometimes unconsciously negotiated by both patient and analyst.* I am suggesting here a type of adaptive or benign iatrogenic resistance. . . . I have in mind complex and lengthy sequences of interaction which only gradually become evident to the analyst as a resistance in the patient and to which the analyst has in some more or less subtle way contributed by his or her own behavior.
>
> (Boesky, 1990, p. 572; emphasis in original)

Going further than Sandler and, I believe, in essential agreement with Tower, Boesky considers these interactive forms of transference resistance, to which the analyst inadvertently contributes, to be a part of every successful analysis and an unavoidable expression of the essential emotional participation of the analyst. He states the matter baldly: "If the analyst does not get emotionally involved sooner or later in a manner that he had not intended, the analysis will not proceed to a successful conclusion" (Boesky, 1990, p. 573).[6]

Transformation and Resisting Transformation

Writing within the American interpersonal tradition, a forerunner of today's relational schools of psychoanalysis, Edgar Levenson's (1972, 1983) concepts of "transformation" and "resisting transformation" are related to the concepts just reviewed. It is an unfortunate byproduct of psychoanalytic politics that his work was not known or cited by the contemporary Freudian theorists, including myself, writing about enactment. Levenson's conception of this aspect of analytic process is as follows: "Most strikingly, and perhaps the single most significant observation for the therapy, whatever the content of the session, it will be simultaneously played out, *choreographed* in the metacommunication of therapist and patient; the formal aspects of the session replicate the content" (1972, pp. 188–89). "[O]ne analyzes . . . the entire piece of living theater they have just played out" (Levenson, 1972, p. 158, emphasis in the original).

Interestingly, Levenson's interpersonal/perspectivist orientation differs from contemporary constructivist and intersubjective theories – and in this regard is more in line with the formulations from the more intrapsychic perspectives just reviewed – in that he regards the patient as the more influential of the two participants in creating an enacted process. In his view, while the analyst's personality and particular responses to the patient are ongoing, it is the patient who inevitably pulls the analyst into an actualization of patient's transference expectations. As he puts it. "In terms of the psychoanalytic situation, no matter what the therapist's starting posture, he will be pulled inexorably into the patient's private universe" (Levenson, 1972, p. 210). "[T]he patterning *emerges from the patient*" (Levenson, 1983, p. 64; emphasis in the original).

Levenson's account of the patient's attempts at "transformation" and the analyst's doomed efforts at "resisting transformation" is thus similar to Sandler's concept of "role responsiveness," Tower's concept of "counter-transference structures," and Boesky's concept of "unconsciously negoti-ated resistance" in their attempts to capture the nature of the play within the play. As do Tower and Boesky, Levenson considers the living out of these treatment versions of the patient's internalized object-relational patterns as inevitable and essential components of analytic process. All four of these theorists also emphasize that analytic change comes about through these relivings *in conjunction with* post-enactment interpretation and working through.

Levenson does seem to differ, however, as to how much of the interactive process is unconscious, and how much is within the analyst's conscious control and a part of his or her technique:

> The function of the therapist is through awareness to resist transformation. Like a continuous discordant note, he shifts the melody. What emerges is still the patient's private myth (not . . . the therapist's) but a myth shifted to account for new data. . . . [The therapist] acts from within the structure of the patient's transactional field – as it were, by being unassimilated. . . . Successful therapy may not be so much a consequence of what the therapist does as it is of what he does not permit to happen.
>
> (1973, pp. 214–15)

Levenson does not address aspects of this process that, for extended periods, may be outside the awareness of the analyst and which thus form an *unconsciously evolving* dimension of the treatment.

Each of the six conceptualizations of the transference–countertransference matrix just reviewed capture aspects of what I conceptualize as the enacted dimension of analytic process – an unconscious, dynamically evolving, transference–countertransference process, unique to each analytic dyad and essential to the therapeutic action of psychoanalysis. They are the forerunners of the concept of enactment, a term coined and developed in the late 1980s by theorists working within a contemporary Freudian framework but one that has become broadly accepted and utilized, if often unclearly defined, by analysts of all orientations. The next chapter will take up "enactment" in an effort to tease out the definitional problems that have led me to propose the concept of the enacted dimension of analytic process.

Notes

1 I prefer the term "transference–countertransference matrix" over the more recent term "two-person psychology" as it more clearly references the unconscious interplay between the psyches of patient and analyst rather than an interpersonal interaction between two "persons." This distinction – between "interpsychic" interaction on the one hand, and interpersonal and intersubjective interaction on the other – will be taken up more fully in Chapter 7.

2 Within his own framework, Sandler (1993) conceptualizes projective identification as a defensive activity with two steps, one intrapsychic and one interpersonal: first is an intrapsychic process of splitting off and projecting (displacing) in unconscious fantasy some unwanted aspect of a self-representation onto an object representation; this is followed by the externalization of the object representation (now revised to include the unwanted aspect of the self) onto an external object (e.g., the analyst) via an actualization process in which the analyst is pushed, through unconscious verbal and nonverbal maneuvers, into playing a particular role vis-à-vis the patient. The analyst's participation constitutes a compromise formation between the patient's pressure and the analyst's own unconscious tendencies.

3 Tower's paper has been little noted, perhaps because her concept of countertransference structure became associated with the controversial concept of "countertransference neurosis," despite her explicit rejection of that concept (see p. 235).

4 In Boesky's perspective, *interaction* is a descriptive term referring only to the locus of the analytic process, still within an intrapsychic framework. He distinguishes his perspective, which continues to emphasize the mutative role of interpretation, from interpersonal, relational, or intersubjective perspectives which, in his view, emphasize the mutative role of the relationship.

5 Boesky's idea of "unconsciously negotiated resistance" thus also differs from Gerson's (1996) concept of "intersubjective resistance" as it does not insist that *all* resistance are co-constructed.

6 A similar idea was expressed by Mitchell (1988): "Unless the analyst affectively enters the patient's relational matrix or, rather, discovers himself within it – unless the analyst is in some sense charmed by the patient's entreaties, shaped by the patient's projections, antagonized and frustrated by the patient's defenses – the treatment is never fully engaged, and a certain depth within the analytic experience is lost" (p. 293).

3

ENACTMENT
The Emergence of a New Concept

My purpose in this chapter is to trace the emergence of the term of enactment, which has now been adopted by analysts of all theoretical schools and persuasions, and to provide an overview of the many varied, and sometimes problematic, ways the phenomenon has been conceptualized and applied clinically. I hope to provide some clarity about this important aspect of analytic process which I believe is better thought of as a continuous *dimension* of all analytic treatment. My conceptualization of this *enacted dimension of analytic process* will be explicated in the next chapter and illustrated throughout the remainder of the book. (For other reviews of the literature on enactment the reader is referred to Aron, 1996; Gabbard, 1995; Hirsch, 1998; Ivey, 2008; Katz, 1998.)

A Brief History of the Term "Enactment"

The term "enactment" was introduced into the psychoanalytic lexicon by Theodore Jacobs in his 1986 paper, "Countertransference Enactments." This paper was the beginning of Jacobs' large body of work devoted to illustrating how the *interplay* between the psychologies of patient and analyst affects the course and outcome of psychoanalytic work. Over the years, through numerous clinical vignettes presented in rich detail and with engaging style, he has illustrated how unintended actualizations in the transference–countertransference matrix create symbolic versions of the patient's core conflicts and object-relational patterns. The concept of enactment now supplements the traditional understanding of transference and countertransference which, while essential, denote too much of an artificial separation from the process by which the patient's unconscious fantasy is brought to life in the unconsciously lived-out drama of the analytic pair.

During the late 1980s and throughout the decade of the 1990s Jacobs (1991, 1994, 1997, 2001a, 2001b) and such theorists as Judith Chused (1991, 1998), Dale Boesky (1990), James McLaughlin (1987, 1991),

Warren Poland (1988, 1992a, 1992b), Owen Renik (1993a), Ralph Roughton (1993, 1994, 1996) and Henry Smith (1993a, 1993b, 1997, 2000), among others, began to further develop the concept of enactment. This strain of Freudian theorists, most of whose roots can be traced to Hans Loewald's developmental and object-relational vision of Freudian theory, has been variously referred to in the literature as the "left wing" of the Freudian spectrum (Druck, 1989), "interactional" Freudians (Aron, 1996; Boesky, 1990; Dunn, 1994), and "modern structural" Freudian theorists (Druck, 2011). These writers expanded contemporary Freudian theory to encompass the kinds of unconscious transference–countertransference processes introduced earlier by the Kleinian, British object-relational, and American theorists reviewed in the last chapter, and too long neglected by early classical theorists.

Also during the late 1980s and the decade of the 1990s several theoretical perspectives, loosely grouped under the heading of relational psychoanalysis, were evolving alongside of the developments in contemporary American Freudian theory just described (see Harris, 2011, for a history and extensive survey of the relational orientation). Prior to the 1990s, during the hegemony of the American Psychoanalytic Association, the antipathy between the classical and interpersonal schools prevented any serious cross-fertilization of ideas. In the changing atmosphere of the 1990s, the relational movement, with its privileging of the interactional aspects of the analytic relationship and, in particular, its focus on the analyst's contribution, provided significant impetus to the expansion of contemporary Freudian theory to more formally include these facets of analytic process.

Regarding enactment in particular, the relational literature has focused attention on the phenomenon's relationship to the concepts of dissociation and multiplicity. Many writers from the relational perspective (see, for example, Benjamin, 2010; Bromberg, 2003, 2006, 2011; Davies, 1998; Davies & Frawley, 1994; D. B. Stern, 2009) view mind as being organized and governed by multiple, dissociated self states, rather than by a dynamic unconscious formed by the motivated repression of, or other defenses against, psychic conflict. The focus on dissociation, regardless of one's view of whether or not it is central in all personality organization, has been particularly useful in our efforts to understand the ways in which trauma, both early sexual and physical abuse and acute adult trauma, is processed by and organized within the personality, and the enacted ways such experiences may then become represented in treatment. The interrelationship of trauma, dissociation, and enactment is the subject of Part III of this book.

The first panel discussion on enactment took place at the 1989 meeting of the American Psychoanalytic Association in San Francisco (Johan, 1992). Participating in the panel were James McLaughlin (Chair), Dale Boesky,

Judith Chused, and Theodore Jacobs, all of whose presentations were subsequently published as individual papers (Boesky, 1989; Chused, 1991; Jacobs, 1991; McLaughlin, 1991).[1]

At that first panel discussion, despite his original emphasis on *counter-transference* enactments (1986), Jacobs employed the term broadly, applying it to any verbal or nonverbal behavior, by either patient or analyst, that actualizes an unconscious wish or defense. He considered them pieces of corrective interactions between therapist and patient that also provide an opportunity for both to gain insights into aspects of their relationship that may not previously have come into focus. He noted that enactments "often express what is not yet otherwise expressible in words. As nonverbal conveyors of rising memories, concealed resistances, and fantasies waiting to see the light of day, they are avant-garde messengers that anticipate and signal what is to come" (Johan, 1992, p. 836).

Chused's use of the term, closely followed by McLaughlin's, was more specific and, at that time, more original. Both restricted the term to inter-actional forms of enactment – that is, to events that actualize unconscious wishes or defenses in *both* patient and analyst. In Chused's terms, an enact-ment is "a symbolic interaction between analyst and patient which has unconscious meaning to *both*" (1991, p. 615; emphasis in the original). She noted that such an interaction was not necessarily behavioral, but could also consist of a nonverbal communication cloaked in words. McLaughlin emphasized events within the analytic relationship that are experienced as interpersonal "happenings," co-constituted by the parties in consequence of shared regression. Each participant, he noted, stirs resonance in the other of old conflicts which between them become actualized for each.

Boesky's definition was similar to Jacobs's in not insisting on there being an interaction. (In his 1990 paper, however, Boesky viewed enactment as unconsciously negotiated by both parties.) He focused on "experiences or behaviors that have an actualizing intention" (Boesky, 1989, p. 3). He emphasized that it was the inner experience of patient and analyst that is essential to the phenomenon – that the behavior derives from the actualization of these experiences. The essential feature, he stated, is "the transformation of ideas and fantasies into a performance which seems real."

All four participants considered enactments ubiquitous and inevitable, and all four agreed that either the patient or the analyst might contribute to an enactment. While having different emphases during the discussion, at the panel's conclusion all four arrived at an agreed upon definition:

> Enactments derive from unconscious sources in both patient and analyst. Enactments are those moments, from brief and single moments to prolonged and/or multiple time periods, during which the patient's action, in the service of transference resistance,

interacts with the analyst's resistance. The analyst's resistance subsumes those phenomena which have been called the analyst's countertransference, counteridentifications, or his transferences to that particular patient. The actions of both patient and analyst may vary from silent withholding and withdrawal to motor action of greater or lesser dramatic notice. While these phenomena have been observed, noted, and described for some time, those present at the panel regarded the term enactment as especially useful because it denotes a two-party interactional situation. That situation is the observable presentation of unconscious meaning residing in both analyst and patient. Enactments, when they can be noticed and raised to consciousness, offer a road to unconscious mental life which might otherwise be left untraversed by the mutual tacit unconscious agreement of analyst and patient.

(Johan, 1992, p. 841)

Thus the term enactment entered the psychoanalytic lexicon in order to conceptualize, within a traditional intrapsychic framework, an aspect of the transference–countertransference matrix in which unconscious issues in the patient and analyst interpenetrate and actualize each other through some form of action between them. It is noteworthy that while the concept of *actualization* was used by each participant in his or her individual presentation, it is not present in the panel's final definition which, instead, emphasized the term *resistance*. This holdover from the earlier concept of acting out, with its negative connotation and its emphasis on motor behavior, foreshadowed the difficulty the new concept has had finding a clear definition (see below).

During the two decades following the 1989 panel, enactment and patient–analyst interaction became a focus of all contemporary schools of psychoanalysis. On the clinical level, the term enactment has now been used countless times in clinical reports and is a welcome addition to our literature, introducing fuller and more complex accounts of analytic process and the interactional aspects of the analytic relationship. On the theoretical level, Boesky (2000, p. 257) notes that, "[Enactment] bridge[s] the interface between what is expressible and inexpressible, between what is forgotten and what is pressing for revival, between reality and fantasy and also between one-person and two-person psychologies. Conceptually the term enactment facilitates the integration of the concepts of fantasy, projective identification and countertransference."

Today's broad-based interest in enactment and transference–countertransference interaction has led Hirsch (1998) to suggest that it represents a partial theoretical convergence between contemporary Freudian and interpersonal/relational theories. Gabbard (1995) has called it the new common ground. There is merit to these assertions only in the broad sense that all orientations now employ the term enactment and all are concerned with exploring the interactive aspects of analytic process. Not only is there is no uniformity about how to define the term enactment, even by analysts working within the same orientation, there is no agreement across orientations about just what is meant by patient–analyst interaction and how much of the patient–analyst interaction should be called enactment.[2] (See Ivey [2008] for a similar view about the absence of theoretical convergence.) The theoretical premises of each analytic orientation lead to different understandings as to what is meant by "co-creation" or "co-construction" of analytic data, and to different ideas as to how, if at all, the phenomenon of enactment affects our approach to analytic technique, or how it contributes to our understanding of therapeutic action (see Bachant et al., unpublished; Louw & Michael, 2001). I will take up these issues in depth in Chapters 7 and 8. At this juncture, I would like to summarize what I see as the main areas of confusion and disagreement that have led to the current unclarity about the concept of enactment.

1. **Discrete Events vs. a Continuous Unconscious Process:** Because the phenomena we are trying to conceptualize come to our attention through unusual events – forgetting a session, for example, or the analyst finding him or herself behaving in some other atypical way toward the patient – much of the clinical literature on enactment tends to give the misleading impression that enactment is a discrete, episodic event rather than an evolving unconscious *process* that is the continuous background of the work of analysis. This problem has been noted by a number of writers: Smith (in Opatow, 1996, p. 643) points out that descriptions of enactments in analytic writings, welcome for providing a more vivid interactive view of the analytic situation, do give the misleading impression that enactments are exceptional events rather than the "continuous background of the work of analysis." Maroda (1998, p. 520) states that "[enactment] is not merely an affectively driven set of behaviors, it is necessarily a repetition of past events that have been buried in the unconscious due to associated unmanageable or unwanted emotion." And Aron (1996, 2003) notes that rather than conveying a sense of continuity and process, "the term enactment too easily implies a discrete event" (1996, p. 213).

Further, because these atypical, seemingly discrete and episodic events are overt behaviors, clinical descriptions often do not clearly differentiate between the interpersonal and the intrapsychic levels of the phenomenon – that is, they do not clearly distinguish the phenomenon's observable manifestation (the "happening") from the unconscious experiences that are being *actualized* in each participant. The term enactment thus tends to be used, by analysts from all orientations, to describe both aspects of the phenomenon without being precise as to which part is being referred to.

Ironically, the fusing of action and actualization is the same problem that befell the early definition of acting out leading to the unfortunate devaluation of action and its lengthy absence from psychoanalytic thinking (reviewed in Chapter 1). As it is with acting out, in an enactment (the two-person version of "acting out") the discrete, observable action – in this case the action *between* analyst and patient – is but the proverbial tip of the unconscious iceberg. In fact, actualization experiences may be occurring, and do occur, without any observable, behavioral action, by either participant. On the patient's side, available clues to the analyst's attitudes, reactions, or values – even gratifications inherent in the analytic process itself or an aspect of "correct" technique – can all have particular meaning to a patient and be silently actualizing an unconscious fantasy or fear. Transference actualizations can even be concealed in a patient's *accurate* perceptions of the analyst and go unnoticed by the analyst, especially when those perceptions coincide with the analyst's own self-representations (Chused, 1992; Roughton, 1993). On the analyst's side, Jacobs (1986) amply demonstrated how unconscious countertransference actualizations may be embedded in every aspect of the analytic method and thereby go unnoticed. The ordinary, everyday, activities of listening, feeling empathy, making an intervention – be it interpreting, self-disclosing, containing, or holding – may all be co-opted by and come under the sway of unconscious conflicts within the analyst.

The definition of enactment thus needs to center on and emphasize the underlying, continuously evolving *unconscious process* in which the patient, and analyst, come to experience an early object-relationship, or a repressed or dissociated experience, as having actually come to life within the transference–countertransference matrix.[3] As I shall illustrate through the clinical examples presented in Parts II and III, the observable, often dramatic, component frequently signals a transformation in, or an end of, the enacted process. It is typically a lagging indicator (to borrow a term from economics) of psychic change that has forged ahead of the conscious awareness of both patient and analyst.

2. The Definition of Interaction: Related to the previous issue – that discussions of enactment often do not clearly differentiate between the observable manifestation of the interactive process and the unconscious experiences that are being actualized in each participant – is the different way theorists think about the very concept of interaction. As I indicated above, I will take up the various concepts that fall under the rubric of psychoanalytic interaction (intersubjectivity, interpersonal interaction, the analytic third, and co-creation) in Chapter 7. As a brief introduction, I will point out here that the conceptualization of transference–countertransference interaction by the "interactional" Freudian theorists who originated the concept of enactment (as well as by the earlier Kleinian and British object-relational theorists reviewed in the last chapter) remains within an essentially intrapsychic framework, with its emphasis on the psychic reality and unconscious experience of each participant. While attending to the two-person aspects of the analytic relationship, these writers do not privilege the interpersonal aspect of analysis over the intrapsychic processes within each participant. Their use of the term "interaction" is in the tradition of the "*inter*psychic" perspective of Hans Loewald (1970, 1980) which explores how unconscious dynamics, situated independently in patient and analyst, are communicated, take shape, and find expression alongside of and/or through even the ordinary verbal interaction of the analytic encounter. (It is these unconscious resonances and inter-penetrations that comprise what I will be calling the enacted dimension of analytic process.) In this view, transference and countertransference actualizations are theoretically separable from any overt interpersonal manifestations. Interpsychic transference–countertransference enmesh-ments are considered but one aspect of the patient's transference and the analyst's countertransference, and but one of several routes to the primary analytic data, which remains the patient's internal psychic reality.

Relational theorists, particularly those who more fully embrace some form of constructivist epistemology, do not tend to emphasize this distinction between the interpersonal and interpsychic levels of patient–analyst interaction nor, therefore, the distinction between the observable manifes-tation of enactment and the separate, underlying, unconscious experiences of transference and countertransference actualization. The idea of tran-sference and countertransference as separable phenomena has, for many (see, for example, Hoffman, 1991, 1992), been replaced by the concepts of intersubjectivity and interactive enactment. All psychoanalytic data, including transference and countertransference themselves, are con-sidered to be co-created or co-constructed, and it is co-created inter-action that is considered the primary, even sole, data and focus of analytic inquiry.

3. **Over-emphasis on the Analyst:** Because of today's broad interest in the analyst's subjectivity, the clinical literature often focuses on countertransference enactment – emphasizing the various ways in which the analyst contributes to enactment, even viewing enactment as something perpetrated by the analyst alone. As noted earlier, attention to the analyst's

subjectivity and its continuous impact on the evolving clinical process was all but absent in early Freudian theory. The integration of the interpsychic perspective into its traditional intrapsychic focus was a needed development and has yielded a more robust theory of clinical process. However, an emphasis on the analyst's subjectivity that leads to a "strong" version of intersubjective theory (what Hanly [1999] called "necessary interactionism") tends to foster a clinical theory of enactment that minimizes the centrality and contribution of active unconscious forces and unconscious fantasies in the patient's mind. As pointed out by Greenberg (2001), in focusing too much on analyzing here-and-now patient–analyst "transactions" relational analysts limit their observational field and lose touch with the dimensions of the patient's experience that are personal and private. Additionally, he points out, when the subjectivity of the analyst and his or her role in shaping the patient's experience is emphasized too exclusively, there is a danger of the analyst wanting to provide the patient a particular kind of new experience.

4. Enactment and Analytic Technique: Some writers do see enactment as something to be stimulated, as something to be incorporated into analytic technique. In general, this is more noticeable among relational theorists, whose praxis is characterized by an overall stance that is more active, interactive, and consciously self-revelatory (noted by Aron, 1996, 2006), and who trace their roots to Ferenczi's (1932, 1933) technical experiments in mutual analysis and to its subsequent evolution in American interpersonal theory. As I shall elaborate more fully in Chapter 8, regardless of theoretical orientation, the phenomenon of enactment is a dynamically *unconscious* process, and thus does not, in and of itself, require or justify an across the board general alteration of analytic stance or technique (though these may be needed for other reasons). Rather, the phenomenon contributes to our understanding of the therapeutic action of psychoanalysis.

5. Emphasis on Harmful Enactments: Some in the literature emphasize the harmful or disruptive potential of enactment. These writers view enactment as essentially an error – a relatively infrequent or episodic failure of analytic technique, even if it can be put to productive use after the fact – rather than an integral component or dimension of analytic process. This is most prominent in, but is not limited to, descriptions of enactment by writers in the Kleinian tradition. This view is partially the result of the Kleinian reliance on the concept of projective identification which, as I discussed earlier, is a process in which the analyst is a *recipient* participant but not involved in its creation. The analyst's even inadvertent participation is thus seen as reflecting a failure of containment and understanding at best and, in the case of overt behavioral enactment, as harmful and leading down the slippery slope toward frame and boundary violations (see for example Steiner, 2006). There is no evidence, however, that the inadvertent and ubiquitous way all analysts come to be enlisted as a participant in the patient's transference drama is the cause of, or necessarily leads to, major boundary violations by the analyst. An enacted process – the actualization of unconscious transference and countertransference fantasies – is inherently neither beneficial nor problematic. It is an inevitable part of analytic process, and as it is with the conscious, verbal manifestations of transference and countertransference, the key factor is whether and how it is treated and used analytically once it becomes conscious.

6. Enactment and Therapeutic Action: What Is Mutative?: Related to the view that enactment is essentially an error by the analyst is the idea that only its retrospective interpretation by the analyst is mutative. This "useful but regrettable" definition views enactment as a ubiquitous and inevitable part of treatment, just not a desirable one nor in and of itself a mutative one. Many from the classical Freudian perspective continue to adhere to this position. Even Chused (1991, 1997, 2003; Chused et al., 1999) maintains that it is the absence of enactment or the withdrawal from enactment that is responsible for therapeutic change. Relational analysts, on the other hand, are more likely to place the emphasis on the other side of the insight–experience continuum – how enactment and enacted processes are mutative in and of themselves. In its extreme, as noted above, this perspective may lead to the view that analytic technique should be altered to maximize their occurrence. As I shall elaborate in the next chapter, and illustrate through the clinical material presented in Parts II and III, the mutative potential of enactment lies in *both* factors, experience *and* insight, which interact and synergize each other in interesting and complex ways. Thus enactment is not only ubiquitous and inevitable, it is also an essential and necessary component of analytic process.

7. Narrow Definitions: Some have given the phenomenon of enactment a narrow or idiosyncratic definition. S. J. Ellman (1998; in Chused et al., 1999), for example, considers enactment to be the result of narcissistic disequilibrium on the part of one or both parties, causing either patient or analyst to insert him or herself into the analytic situation in a more real manner. For Ellman, such a break in an analyst's optimal analytic attitude is an indication of an absence or disruption in what he has termed "analytic trust" (2007, 2010). While narcissistic disequilibrium and the breakdown of analytic trust are valuable explanatory concepts, particularly when considering the treatment of more disturbed patients, limiting the definition of *enactment* to these issues overly emphasizes enactment as a disruption or impasse in analytic process and does not address how, as an inevitable dimension of *every* treatment, enacted processes contribute to the essential reliving of the patient's core transference issues.

8. Categorization of Enactment: Others have sought to categorize different types of enactment. For example, Bass (2003, in a discussion of a clinical case presentation by Black, 2003) distinguishes between what he calls "ordinary quotidian" (small e) enactment, and (capital E) Enactment. As described by Bass, the former are more in the background, forming the daily ebb and flow of analytic process, while the latter are events that are so out of the ordinary that they "mobilize our full, heightened attention and define, and often take hold of, our analytic activity for periods of time" (2003, p. 660). Bass's first category, or definition, is so broad as to encompass almost everything that occurs in analytic process (as he notes: "Every interaction between analyst and patient may be usefully viewed as a transference–countertransference enactment" [2003, p. 660]), thereby depriving the concept of unique meaning or necessity. Enactment is not the only thing that transpires in the transference–countertransference matrix. Bass's second category – capital E Enactment – overly highlights discrete atypical events and under-emphasizes the underlying unconscious processes. Positing two different categories of enactment misses the point that small e and capital E enactments are in actuality two aspects of the same phenomenon. As I noted above, and as the clinical case material in Parts II and III will illustrate, a "capital E Enactment" is likely to turn out to be the overt component or manifestation of an "ordinary quotidian" enactment that has been going on for an extended, dynamically meaningful, length of time.

My introduction of the concept of the enacted *dimension* of analytic process (Katz, 1998, 2002, 2011) was intended to provide a conceptual framework for addressing the unsettled issues of definition, technique, and therapeutic action just outlined, and to better capture the evolutionary quality of the patient's internal world as it plays itself out – a process that can evolve over months and even years – within the transference–countertransference matrix. The enacted dimension will be described, elaborated, and illustrated throughout the remainder of this book.

Notes

1 Some of the citations in the following paragraphs are from the individually published papers.

2 As wryly noted by S. J. Ellman (1998, p. 183) over a decade ago, "The term enactment follows a long psychoanalytic tradition in being an important concept with no agreed upon definition." The lack of definitional consensus continues today.

3 This feature of an enacted process, the sense of immediacy and affective aliveness it provides, is also emphasized by Chused (1991) and by Maroda (1998).

Part II

THE ENACTED DIMENSION OF ANALYTIC PROCESS

Viewed as a dramatic play, the transference neurosis is a fantasy creation woven from memories and imaginative elaborations of present actuality, the present actuality being the psychoanalytic situation, the relationship of patient and analyst.

(Loewald, 1975, p. 279)

Thus the therapist and the patient each seeks to behave and to misbehave according to the rules of the inner play. It is as if there is a play within a play, and the transference/countertransference dilemma gives dialectical depth and balance to the other play.

(Grotstein, 1990, p. 175)

The play's the thing
wherein I'll catch the conscience of the king.

(William Shakespeare, 1623,
Hamlet, Act II, Scene II)

4

WHERE THE ACTION IS
The Second Dimension of Analytic Process

In all treatments, a new version – what Freud (1905) called "a new edition" and what Poland (1992) has termed "an original creation" – of the patient's early traumas, conflicts, and formative object relationships is inevitably created, without awareness or intent, in the here and now of the analytic dyad. This new treatment version may evolve over long stretches of time, sometimes years, only becoming available for verbal symbolization and reflective, analytic use at unconsciously determined meaningful junctures in the treatment process. This process takes place in what I have called the treatment's *enacted dimension*. Analytic process thus comprises two interwoven dimensions: the more familiar verbally symbolized dimension (free-association, self-reflection, dream analysis, interpretation, etc.), and the enactively symbolized dimension in which nonverbal communications and unintended actualizations of unconscious and dissociated experience are continuously taking place. These are not dichotomous dimensions or processes, but are inextricably interwoven at all times: the transference–countertransference matrix is continuously evolving on both the enacted and the verbal levels simultaneously. In the enacted dimension, patients will inevitably induce the analyst into playing a part in, and thereby actualizing, an unconscious object relationship or a dissociated traumatic event. This process is more than projection or projective-identification alone, because it specifically includes the involvement of the *analyst's* unconscious in its creation.

These spontaneous creations in analytic space are crucial ingredients of the therapeutic action of psychoanalysis, because, as Freud said long ago, "One cannot overcome an enemy who is absent or not within range" (1914, p. 152) . . . "We must treat the patient's illness," he said, "not as an event of the past, but as a present day force" (1914, p. 150). In an enacted process, the past is not just remembered, it is relived: past experience and current experience become linked with an immediacy and affective vitality that inspires enormous conviction. When these actualization processes become conscious, they form the basis for experientially based interpretive work in the verbal dimension of the treatment, creating the kind of *experiential insight* that produces meaningful psychoanalytic change.

That there should be such an enacted dimension of analytic process should not surprise us. After all, we learn to communicate in action far earlier than we learn to communicate in language, and, as cognitive neuroscientists tell us (reviewed briefly in Chapter 1 and addressed more fully later in this chapter and in Part III), the early, formative experiences of our childhood tend to be encoded in preverbal, sensorimotor forms of memory rather than in verbally accessible representational forms of memory. It is to be expected then that, in analysis, the formative events and experiences of the patient's life will be remembered and more powerfully revived in the same cognitive currency in which they were first laid down. Moreover, the regressive constraints of the analytic frame, in which ordinary actions and visual communication are curtailed, potentiate an intensification of the action intent of words, silences, actions, and nonverbal communications in *both* parties. Thus the analyst may come to discover that he or she, without conscious awareness or intent, has been playing a part in the patient's enacted drama. Such enacted recreations are what Fred Busch (1989) has called "memories in action," and they are an inevitable and necessary component of analytic treatment.

In the context of the interactive, interpsychic, evolution of the transference–countertransference matrix (which I will develop further in Chapter 7), the dual dimensionality of analytic process I am putting forward allows us to recast and supplement our understanding of the more traditional components of analytic process (transference, counter-transference, optimal analytic attitude and technique) and the nature of therapeutic action, as follows.

Analytic Process

The patient's unconscious early formative experiences inexorably press for *actualization* in the treatment setting. This relentless movement from what is repressed or dissociated to its expression in the clinical setting occurs in both the verbally symbolized dimension (through thoughts and fantasies) and in the enacted dimension (through a variety of enacted processes). As Freud noted in his discussion of the repetition compulsion, "The unconscious – that is to say, the 'repressed' . . . has no other endeavor than to break through the pressure weighing down on it and force its way either to consciousness or to a discharge through some real action" (1920, p. 19). Sandler (1976) points out that this is a normal part of all object relations in which an individual unconsciously scans objects and their reactions in the process of object choice, entering into them first in "trial" form and then choosing objects that will fulfill the complementary role.

In analytic treatment, the early formative experiences that are inexorably pressing for actualization are the major contributors to the way the patient organizes (in both "accurate" and "distorted" fashion) his or her experience of the analyst. That is, the patient will continuously utilize real aspects of the analyst's personality, his or her technique, as well as the physical setting and its emotional climate, in the service of actualizing unconscious needs and wishes and the internal object relationships in which they are embedded. These unconscious fantasies and internal object-relational patterns, what the patient "transfers" into the analytic relationship, gradually develop into a coherent, analyzable "transference" as they achieve, whether for brief or extended periods, some meaningful actualization in the enacted dimension of the treatment. The technical suggestion to allow transference manifestations to develop and deepen before interpreting can be conceptualized as the desirability of allowing them to achieve some measure of actualization in the "interactive analytic space" (Poland, 1992a) of the treatment.

The analyst's efforts to maintain a relatively consistent analytic attitude and analytic frame – analytic technique in its broadest sense – is the dialectical counterpart to the patient's press toward transference actualization. It is a balancing force gradually guiding the expression of transference wishes, with attention and sensitivity to the patient's narcissistic vulnerabilities, toward verbal symbolization. Optimal analytic technique maintains for the patient a delicate balance, in the "playground of the treatment," between the actualization of transference and the analysis of transference. This allows the patient's participation in the treatment process to oscillate optimally along a dynamic continuum between, at one pole, the enacted representation of transference and, at the other, its self-reflective verbal symbolization.

Of course, "optimal" analytic technique is only the mean around which the analyst's subjective processes – his or her facilitating emotional involvement as well as unconscious conflicts that interfere with empathy and understanding – continuously revolve. Both will become enlisted in the interactive dynamics of the transference–countertransference matrix, and both may find their expression in the unconscious enacted dimension of the treatment. However, an unconscious intrusion of the analyst's "irreducible" subjectivity will not *necessarily* become a part of an enacted process or have significant impact on the treatment process. The enacted dimension is an unconscious realm of analytic treatment in which a *particular* dynamic or conflict in the analyst becomes relevant to the *particular* patient – usually but not necessarily because it is elicited by the patient – resulting in an actualization of an unconscious conflict, organizing fantasy, trauma, or traumatic internal object-relationship in the patient and, usually to a lesser extent, in the analyst.

Therapeutic Action

Throughout psychoanalytic history, approaches to the question of what is mutative about what we do — what it is that actually helps patients — have, unfortunately, tended to be dichotomized along theoretical/political lines. For example, there is the belief, generally associated with Freudian analysis, that psychic change occurs through insight gained via transference interpretation; there is also the belief, generally associated with relational analysis, that change occurs through new experience within the analytic relationship. This dichotomy is related to another, the one between one-person and two-person models of mind. Both of these polarizations are unfortunate. Regarding insight versus experience, in actuality both operate together and potentiate each other. Insights are often needed in order for new experiences to register as truly new and break free of the sway of transference; new experiences, both inside and outside the treatment, often promote insight (see Jacobs, 1993). And, in my opinion, one-person *and* two-person models are *both* valuable and informative perspectives on the treatment process. The conceptualization of the dual dimensionality of the treatment process presented here illustrates the therapeutic interweaving of insight and experience, as well as the need for both one-person and two-person perspectives, as follows:

In an enacted process, the patient's unconscious world of self and object representations (a one-person perspective) comes to life in the unconsciously experienced enacted dimension of the treatment relationship (a two-person perspective). (Again, by "two-*person*" I refer not to two *people* and their *overt* interactions; I am referring to what Loewald called the *interpsychic* component of that interaction — the unconscious effect each psyche has on the other.) When this unconscious interactive process finally becomes available for conscious reflection, the primary focus is the one-person perspective, that of the patient's experience. The process of therapeutic action here is as follows: the patient first has the *experience* of the analyst's becoming his or her old object (which the analyst inadvertently does to an extent) and then, via the symbolizing and interpretive function of the analyst, the patient has the experience of the analyst's becoming a new therapeutic object. (At first a partly old and partly new object, gradually becoming ever more new and ever less colored by transference.) The analyst's interpretations at this point not only convey content (insight), *they are also themselves new object-relational experiences.* Experience *and* insight operate *together* to promote the kind of emotionally based experiential insight that produces meaningful psychoanalytic change. Jacobs (1991, 1993) has consistently emphasized the value of such "integrative experiences" (Loewald, 1960) in psychoanalytic treatment, and this view is inherent in what Chused (1996) has called "informative experiences" and what Steingart (1995) has termed "insightful experiences."

Neurobiological Correlates

Work being done by researchers in contemporary cognitive neuroscience has been producing some interesting parallels to the idea of a dual dimensionality to psychoanalytic treatment that I have been outlining. MRIs and PET scans reveal that there are two independent, but nevertheless intertwined, neurobiological systems that encode our environmental experiences (Bucci, 1997, 2011a, 2011b, 2011c). One is the *sub-symbolic (or nonsymbolic) organization,* mediated by the thalamic–amygdalar centers, that encodes input from the environment in visceral, motoric, and sensory forms, and then automatically sends them on to the emotion executing sites and to the symbolic processing sites of the higher level *symbolic organization.* This second system, the symbolic organization, is situated in the association areas of the cortex and the memory areas of the hippocampus, and it is the system that creates meaning and language and regulates emotion.

I will have more to say about these two neurobiological systems and their relation to our understanding of dissociative responses to overwhelming trauma in Chapter 11. At this point I wish to point out (without implying that we can directly map our psychoanalytic concepts to physical structures and processes in the brain [see Vivona, 2009a], or that either mode of experience, whether conceptualized on the brain level or on the psychological level, should be considered primary) that the *subsymbolic* and *symbolic* systems are a neurobiological analog to what Loewald, in a 1976 paper on memory, called the *primary memorial system,* where nonrepresentational, enactive forms of memory are stored, and the *secondary memorial system,* where verbally accessible representational forms of memory are stored. In analytic therapy, these two brain systems are the neurobiological analog to the enacted and verbal dimensions of the treatment.

Cognitive neuroscientists also tell us that the neural pathways to the nonsymbolic centers are much faster and stronger than those to the symbolic centers. This explains why the overwhelming affects of early traumatic events are so quickly and easily triggered when the individual perceives that a contemporary situation might be similarly dangerous. Further, because the higher level symbolic centers never became fully engaged at the time of the trauma, the affects and the visceral, sensorimotor responses to the trauma remained disconnected from conscious thought and control, rendering the individual unable to learn new, more adaptive responses.

It is for these reasons that the enacted dimension is such an essential and crucial part of analytic treatment. For after they are reexperienced in this realm of the treatment, the disconnected, or dissociated, aspects of the patient's early trauma can be reintegrated into consciousness, creating new opportunities, on the neurobiological level, to strengthen the neural pathways to the higher order symbolic systems, and on the psychological level, to effect what we analysts call structural change – the kind of change in psychic organization that leads to a more integrated sense of self and a greater capacity for relationships with others.

The next two chapters offer three clinical vignettes from the literature that illustrate the enacted dimension of analytic process.

5

CLINICAL ILLUSTRATIONS I
Reliving Preverbal and Unformulated Experience in the Enacted Dimension

The two vignettes from the literature presented in this chapter, as well as the vignette to be presented in the next chapter, illustrate how the enacted dimension constitutes a continuous, unconscious backdrop to the day-to-day work of analysis. Within this second dimension of the treatment process, without the awareness or intent of either party, preverbal and nonverbal experience find shape and expression. The vignettes illustrate how this *in vivo* treatment version of the early relationships and events that shaped the patient's personality offers the potential for previously unformulated experience to be reintegrated into the fabric of the patient's internal world and external life.

While my main purpose in presenting these vignettes is to bring the theoretical concept of the enacted dimension to life, they also highlight the centrality of the enacted dimension in the treatment of the sequellae of psychic trauma. The enacted dimension is that realm of analytic process where all experiences that cannot be symbolized in words – not only those that are preverbal and have no words, but also those whose overwhelming nature necessitated their dissociation or disavowal – find their expression. Part III will take up several theoretical issues related to trauma and dissociation, and illustrate the enacted dimension of three detailed case presentations.

Vignette 1: The Tissue Box Enactment

In his paper on role responsiveness, Joseph Sandler (1976) describes a patient whose chronic anxiety required her to structure her world so as to always feel in control. From the beginning of the treatment, she cried regularly in sessions, which elicited from Sandler the response of regularly handing her a box of tissues. Sandler states that he did not know why he was doing this (he did not do the same with other patients), but he decided not to alter it or bring it up until he understood it better. Then, one day, two and a half years later (remember that time frame), the patient begins to cry but Sandler finds himself *not* passing her the tissues, and again not knowing why. The patient upbraids him for callously abandoning her. Sandler says to her that he doesn't know why he did not pass the tissues, but if they could continue talking about it, perhaps it would become clearer.

The ensuing analysis of this interaction uncovered memories that clarified that the patient's underlying anxiety began following her mother's withdrawal upon the birth of her brother, when she was two and a half. The patient feared soiling or wetting herself and there being no mother around to clean her up. According to Sandler, the patient had unconsciously elicited in him an *actualizing role enactment* (which he defines as partly induced by the patient, and also partly a product of the analyst's own unconscious dynamics) – in which he became, initially, the mother who cleaned her up and then the mother who did not.

Thus, for the entire two-and-a-half-year period of treatment reported – side by side with the day-to-day work in the verbally symbolized dimension that we commonly, perhaps too simplistically, consider *the* analytic process – a crucial drama was taking place, unawares, in the enacted dimension of the treatment. The first part of this interaction, experienced by the patient as the transference actualization of the mother who cleaned her up, held in abeyance the transference reexperience of the traumatic childhood event. The second part of the interaction, experienced by the patient as the actualization of the trauma itself, took place at a point in the treatment – after two and half years – when the patient had experienced the analyst as a caretaking mother for the symbolically meaningful period.

Now: what is the "enactment" here? It is not simply the interpersonal action of passing (or not passing) the tissue box. More accurately, it is the continuous stream of unconscious transference–countertransference communications and actualizations that were going on right from the treatment's inception. In fact, as is often the case, the dramatic behavioral or interpersonal event (Sandler's suddenly failing to pass the tissue box) was, in fact, the *endpoint* of the underlying actualization processes, a "lagging indicator" (to borrow a term from economics) of psychic change that had *already occurred* in the treatment process, psychic change that had forged ahead of both the patient's and the analyst's awareness. Through the enacted process, Sandler's patient had become ready to create and experience a new version of the original trauma in the treatment, which she unconsciously communicated to her analyst, who unconsciously received it. The dramatic, overt component of the enacted process – failing to pass the tissue box – was, in effect, a wake-up call that summoned the analyst to recognize that the enacted and verbally symbolized dimensions of the treatment were now ready for integration.

44

Vignette 2: The Hostile Interpretation

The second vignette, from an early paper by Owen Renik (1993a, pp. 144–49), concerns the two-year treatment of a timid, inhibited man who was inwardly boiling with rage, particularly at women. The treatment had been going well up this point but had recently begun to bog down. One day the patient announced that he had not taken any sleeping pills, which he used occasionally, for a month. He complained that "it was like being weaned from the breast" – the analyst could not possibly know how difficult it was. Renik makes the following comment: "It's as if you feel like the only person who was ever weaned from the breast."

Renik reports that while the comment was accurate – calling the patient's attention to attitudes of entitlement and a sense of injustice that were central features of the transference – it was made in the context of his feeling frustrated with the pace of the treatment and impatient with the patient's whiny complaints, both of which had stimulated what Renik describes as his own grandiose self-pity. As a result, the interpretation was "not entirely kindly meant, and therefore was not put as gently as it might have been."

Neither patient nor analyst addresses the hostility expressed in the interpretation. The patient merely acknowledges the truth of its content and compliantly associates to it. However, a clue to his warded-off unconscious experience of the interaction breaks through in a slip: he substitutes the name "Gary" for the name of his son. When asked about this, he said: "The only Gary I can think of is the younger brother my parents told me about that was stillborn when I was a year and a half old." The patient had never before mentioned this fact. The slip leads to the retrieval of the following important early childhood information: following the stillbirth, the mother had suffered a severe postpartum depression and the patient was sent to live with his aunt for six months. In exchange for his not contradicting his aunt's fantasy that he was her son, she was unconditionally accepting of him, enabling him to ward off experiencing the traumatic rejection by his mother.

So let's look at the *enacted dimension* of this analytic process. As pointed out by Renik, right from the beginning of the treatment, patient and analyst were duplicating, unawares, the patient's childhood relationship with his aunt. In the treatment's enacted dimension – alongside the ongoing day-to-day work of the analysis in the verbally symbolized sphere – the patient was experiencing his analyst's patient attention and therapeutic optimism as an actualization of the aunt's all-accepting love for him; and the analyst was experiencing the patient's initial eager cooperation and progress as a confirmation of what Renik describes in the paper as his own "grandiose expectation" that he would be allowed to succeed where all others had failed.

At a certain point, two years into the treatment – I remind the reader that the patient was a year and a half old when he was sent to the aunt and was with her for half a year – the pace of psychological discovery and symptomatic improvement slowed, and mutual disappointment set in. The analyst's angry disappointment, expressed via the hostile interpretation, now actualized for the patient the disavowed rejection by his depressed mother: he experienced the analyst as punishing him for all the hostility and demands that lurked beneath his good-patient pose, just as he felt his devastated mother had sent him away because of the resentment and frustration he felt he had to endure during her pregnancy and for his jealous rage toward his unborn sibling that he imagined had caused the stillbirth.

There are several things of note in these two vignettes: First, both treatments required an extensive period for the trauma to achieve symbolic actualization within the transference–countertransference matrix, during which time neither patient nor analyst was aware of the meaning and analytic significance of what they were recreating. In fact, in both vignettes, the new treatment edition of the preverbal trauma took the same length of time to unfold as did the original trauma – two and a half years for Sandler's patient and two years for Renik's patient. I have found this kind of time-frame recapitulation to occur in many of the clinical presentations I have been asked to discuss. When I point this out, however, many people react as if this were merely coincidence, pure speculation on my part. (I have even been accused of practicing a specious form of numerology, the kind that can lose you a lot of money at a racetrack.) Even Sandler, in his own discussion of his vignette, parenthetically states: "It would be pure speculation to link the two and a half years of analysis with the age when her anxiety started" (1976, p. 47). I am not sure why there is skepticism about this idea. After all, we are all aware of and believe in what are called "anniversary reactions." Clearly, the unconscious can keep track, in its own timeless way, of significant events of the past and then make them feel immediate and alive in the present. Can we not view what transpired in the enacted dimension of these two treatments as a kind of elaborate anniversary reaction, an extended reliving induced by the regression fostered by analytic treatment?

I have found that such elaborate chronological recapitulations in the enacted dimension (which probably occur more often than we realize) are especially common when it is a specific early trauma that is being unconsciously "remembered." Because the original experience was so overwhelming that it needed to be warded off in its entirety, it can only become available to consciousness after being recreated and relived in its original entirety. It is only then, at the symbolically meaningful point in the process, that it becomes available for verbal symbolization and integration. (See Part III for further illustrations of how trauma may be reexperienced in the enacted dimension.) This is not to say that there aren't other kinds of enacted processes that are less bound by a repetition of a specific duration. Because the enacted dimension is a continuous background aspect of the transference–countertransference matrix, non-time-frame enactments – more accurately, *actualizations of unconscious fantasy* – are always occurring in an ongoing way and are thus the rule rather than the exception. They are simply not sexy enough to make a journal article.

Second, Renik's hostile interpretation was not simply counter-transference, nor was it in and of itself "the enactment." Rather, the hostile interpretation, like Sandler's *not* passing the tissue box, was the culmination of the treatment-long, transference–countertransference *process* taking place in the enacted dimension of the treatment. Within this enacted drama, Renik's intervention, like Sandler's, came at a moment when his patient had become ready to fully reexperience his trauma in the treatment, and his analyst – for unconscious reasons of his own – was ready to be enlisted to play the necessary part in his patient's unconsciously orchestrated drama. However, *unlike* Sandler's passing and then failing to pass the tissue box, the enacted process in the Renik vignette involved no unusual behavioral action. The transference and countertransference actualizations were embedded and disguised in ordinary analytic technique throughout the entire treatment – initially, in the productive analytic work both parties found gratifying, and then in the routine analytic activity of making an interpretation. Thus, over and above the meaning he consciously intended them to convey, Renik's words – influenced by unconscious pressures from both sides of the couch – became just as much a concrete behavior as was Sandler's. As James McLaughlin put it, words can be "sticks or stones, hugs or holdings" (1987, p. 598).

Third, in the Renik vignette, thanks to his account of his own countertransference issues and the unique way they actualized the patient's traumatic history, we can clearly see how two *separate* intrapsychic dramas can interpenetrate and actualize each other in the enacted dimension of the treatment as well as how, despite this co-created aspect, the analytic focus remained on the unique meaning the enacted process had for the patient. (I will have more to say about the concept of co-creation in Chapter 7, and about the relationship between enactment and analytic technique in Chapter 8.) The work with the patient did not dwell on the analyst's countertransference nor on the transference–countertransference co-createdness. Rather, after the experience in the enacted dimension became conscious, the analytic work focused on the *patient's* early history and trauma as it had come to be lived-out in the treatment, providing him with what I earlier referred to as a unique kind of *experiential insight*. This is not simply insight about the past; it is insight about a past that is palpably alive in the present. In an enacted process, the patient doesn't just have a past, he is his past. Nor is the experience simply *an experience with a new, "better" object.* Rather, it is *a new experience with an "old" object – the original internal object* (see Loewald, 1960). The reactivation of the dissociated, split-off trauma in the enacted dimension of the treatment relationship now afforded Renik's patient the opportunity, via the analytic work in the verbal dimension, to begin the process of reintegrating it. This would include the analysis and working through of the fantasy constellations that colored the internal representations of his split maternal objects, and the layers of conflict and compromise formation in which they later became embedded. The patient could now begin, gradually, and for the first time, to forge ways of relating to these, until now separate, internal objects – the all-loving aunt and the rejecting, traumatizing mother – making possible new ways of understanding and experiencing himself and more adaptive and satisfying relationships, particularly with women, in his current life. In short, within the enacted dimension of the treatment, the patient converted the trauma that he had been forced to endure *passively* in childhood into something that he *actively* (albeit unconsciously) *intended,* thereby creating for himself the opportunity, within this "new edition" of the trauma, to actively master it. This is quite different from a consciously intended attempt to provide the patient with a corrective relationship with a new, better object.

6

CLINICAL ILLUSTRATIONS II

An Enacted Process Within an Enacted Process

Patrick Casement's 1982 paper, "Some Pressures on the Analyst for Physical Contact During the Re-living of an Early Trauma," is one of the more frequently cited papers in analytic literature when it comes to discussions of the abstinence principle and physical contact between patient and analyst. In my 1998 paper, I discussed the vignette presented in his paper from the standpoint of what I saw as its enacted dimension. Subsequently, this treatment case became the focus of a 2000 issue of *Psychoanalytic Inquiry* devoted to the issue of touch. In the course of his discussion of the contributions made by the eight discussants of his original paper, Casement supplied additional details about the case. The new information revealed a second level of enacted process beneath the one I had originally discussed. In this chapter I will present both my original discussion of this treatment's enacted dimension, as well as the second level of enacted process that lay beneath it.

Mrs. B

In the original paper, Casement describes the analysis of a young woman, Mrs. B, who had been seriously scalded in an accident at the age of 11 months. Six months later, she was operated on to release the scar tissue from the surrounding skin. During the operation (performed under local anesthesia), her mother, who was present and holding her hand, fainted – falling to the ground and releasing her daughter's hand. The surgeon continued the procedure despite the mother's collapse.

In reliving this experience in the treatment, following a summer break, the patient reported a dream about a despairing ten-month-old child and requested that she be allowed to hold the analyst's hand lest her anxiety become intolerable. In a Friday session, the patient threatened that unless she were able to hold the analyst's hand she would not continue the analysis. Casement managed this crisis by saying to her that some analysts would not contemplate allowing this but that he realized she might need to have the *possibility* of holding his hand if it seemed the only way for her to get through this experience. In this way he kept open the possibility of granting her request, as well as the opportunity for further analytic work.

Over the intervening weekend he reassessed the situation and realized that he was in part reacting to his own fear of losing the patient (he was about to present a paper about her to his society). More critically, however, he realized that to allow her to hold his hand would not help her to get through a reexperiencing of the original trauma, which had involved the *absence* of the mother's hand, and would only reinforce her perception that what she was going through was something too terrible ever fully to be remembered or to be experienced. As a result of this analysis of the situation, he decided to review with his patient the implications of his offer.

Over the same weekend, the analyst received a hand-delivered letter from the patient informing him that she had had another dream about a despairing child, but that this time the child was crawling toward a motionless figure with the excited expectation of reaching the figure. In Monday's session, the patient explained that she had been afraid the analyst might collapse over the weekend if he had to wait until Monday to be reassured that she was feeling more hopeful. She then reported another image: when the child reaches the figure and touches it, it crumbles and collapses. At this point the analyst explained to her his rethinking, why he had decided that he should not hold her hand. The patient was devastated, assuming he could not bear to be in touch with what she was going through.

Casement then describes in sensitive detail the elaboration of the transference reliving, which hovered precariously for several weeks between delusion and workable illusion before its final resolution. At one point, the patient developed the delusion that the analyst was actually her mother and demanded to be held. Casement states that it was meaningless to her when he tried to interpret this "as transference, as a reliving of her childhood experience . . . there seemed to be no remaining contact with me as analyst" (1982, p. 282).

At this critical juncture, Casement states, he finally became aware of the patient's projective identification – that he had been feeling her despair and helplessness and the impossibility of going on – and was able to interpret from his countertransference feelings. He said to her, "I feel as if it could be impossible to go on, yet I feel that the only way I can help you through this is by being prepared to tolerate what you are making me feel, and going on" (1982, p. 283).

Following this intervention, the patient began to speak to Casement as the analyst again, and actually had the sensation of smelling and feeling the hands of her pre-trauma mother's presence. She was able finally to accept his original interpretations: that her wish for him to concretely hold her hands was a wish for him to really be in touch with what she was going through and that, had he agreed, he would have become a collapsed mother/analyst. She expressed gratitude that he did not allow this to happen.

The Enacted Dimension

In my original discussion of this skillfully managed and productive clinical process (Katz, 1998), I described its enacted dimension as follows. The clinical sequence begins "soon after the summer holiday," with a dream about a ten-month-old despairing child, and builds in intensity until the crisis about the request to hold the analyst's hand takes place during a Friday session, before a weekend separation. Thus, the transference reliving of the infantile trauma, utilizing the real separations in the analytic (hand-) holding environment (the enacted dimension of the treatment), brought about an intense transference evocation to actualize an *undoing* of the trauma. This took overt form in the patient's demand to hold the analyst's hand. The analyst's initial equivocation was a compromise formation fashioned out of his role-responsiveness to this transference evocation and his own countertransference overidentification with the patient's fear of devastating separation and loss – in the analyst's case, fear over losing his relationship with his analytic society (connected, no doubt, to other issues at deeper levels). Over the weekend separation, the patient extended *her* hand to the analyst (the *hand*-delivered letter containing her hopeful dream) to prevent his fantasied "collapse" – an enacted attempt to undo her fantasied destruction of the analyst/mother during the weekend separation.

Upon being reunited in the Monday session, the patient reported that the figure in the dream crumbled and collapsed when the child touched it. Precisely at this point in the session the analyst decided to explain to the patient his rethinking of her request to hold his hand. The comment's timing – in part a reaction formation against the continuing countertransference wish to grant the patient's request – actualizes the patient's transference fear that her intense need had caused her mother's collapse/destruction. The analyst's attempt to interpret the ensuing delusional experience "as transference, as a reliving of her childhood experience," did not ameliorate the situation: "there seemed to be no remaining contact with me as analyst." I believe this was so because the analyst was still involved in the partial actualization of his own concordant countertransference (Racker, 1957), which had interpenetrated with the patient's intense transference evocation. (In Casement's terms, he had accepted the patient's projective identification.)[1] As a result, the interpretation, though correct, was only a flat intellectual reiteration of a known historical event (the mother's fainting and dropping out of sight) rather than a living interpretation centering on the patient's actual(ized) experience of the analyst's withdrawal of the hand-holding possibility and his subsequent absences over the weekends – the interactive enacted process.

When the analyst finally realized that he had been overidentified with the patient's terror of experiencing catastrophic loss, he was able to effectively interpret *within* the "original creation" transference. The analyst's crucial comment – that he was prepared to tolerate what the patient was making him feel – repositioned him as the mother who could tolerate her terror without fainting (faltering in his analytic function), thereby affording her a transference experience that disconfirmed her unconscious expectations. This entire enacted process could then be brought within the verbally symbolized dimension of the transference – an aspect of working through – leading to the attainment of authentic insight and "higher psychical organization" (Freud, 1915b, p. 202).

The Second Level of the Enacted Dimension

In his discussion of the case in the 2000 issue of *Psychoanalytic Inquiry,* Casement provides details about the patient's burns that neither he nor Mrs. B knew at the time of the analysis (the patient learned of it from her mother only after her treatment) nor at the time the original paper was written. At the time the patient was burned, the doctor had informed her mother that it would not have been safe for the patient to be transferred to the nearest hospital for treatment. The only hospital she could have gotten to was known then to be in no fit state to care for a patient with such severe burns, and the doctor actually thought that the child would die if she were to be sent to that hospital. In consideration of these facts, the doctor told the patient's mother that the best chance of her child's surviving would be if the mother could nurse her in the home. But that would mean "barrier nursing" her, which meant *not holding her or touching her* except with sterilized gloves and sterilized implements and then only for the most minimal and essential feeding and cleaning of the child. Whatever she did, the mother must not pick up her baby – however much the baby cried to be picked up – for if the mother did pick up her baby, it might lead to her dying from infection. In the paper, Casement comments on the remarkable parallel with what was recreated in the treatment:

> What a parallel! So, we can imagine the agonies that her mother must have gone through as she cared for her baby, while having to inhibit the natural impulse of a mother to hold her distressed baby to herself, to give her the hug that is meant to "make it all better." Strangely, and I had no inkling of this at the time, I too had to go

through similar agonies in being there for my patient's distress, and readers of my description of this [in the *Psychoanalytic Inquiry* issue] also seem to have sensed something of that agony, wishing so strongly that my patient could at least have had the reassurance of my hand to help her through that experience. And, at the time, what I was doing made no more sense to Mrs. B (consciously) than it has to those discussants who have so much disagreed with my handling of this case; yet the main thing that got me through that awful time (and it was many months before it began to feel at all better – to Mrs. B or to me) was my awareness of my patient's unconscious communications to me. There it was that I had been prompted to see the implications of this choice and to see what was required of me at this point in the analysis.

(Casement, 2000, p. 179)

If we look back at the clinical process reported in the original 1982 paper, we can see that what was being relived and reexperienced in the enacted dimension of the treatment was not only the mother's fainting and dropping her hand at the surgery but also the more traumatic barrier nursing that had occurred earlier: the total and protracted loss of contact with her mother. Following are direct quotes from the original paper (1982, pp. 281–83. All italicized text is in the original; underlined text is my highlights):

She dreamed of *being very small and being denied the only food she wanted. It was there but a tall person would not let her have it.*

In the second dream *she was falling through the air, convinced that she was going to die despite the fact that she was held by a parachute with a helicopter watching over her.* She could see the contradictions (sure of dying whilst actually being safe) but this did not stop her feeling terrified in the dream, and still terrified of me in the session. She stressed that she didn't know if I realized that she was still feeling sure that she was dying inside.

The next day the patient felt that she was going insane. She had dreamed *there was a sheet of glass between herself and me so that she couldn't touch me or see me clearly. It was like a car wind-screen with no wipers in a storm.* I interpreted her inability to feel that I could get in touch with what she was feeling, because of the barrier between her and me created by the storm of her feelings inside her ... She agreed and collapsed into uncontrolled crying, twisting on the couch, tortured with pain. At the end of this session she became panicked that I wouldn't be able to tolerate having experienced this degree of her distress.

The next week Mrs. B continued to say that she didn't think she could go on. She had had many terrible dreams over the week-end. The following day she again sat up for the session. For much of this session she seemed to be quite deluded. Awareness of reality was fleeting and tenuous. For the greater part of the session she was a child. <u>She began by saying she didn't just talk to her baby, she picks him up and holds him</u>. Then, looking straight at me she said "I am a baby and you are the person I need to be my mother. I need you to realize this, because unless you are prepared to hold me I cannot go on. You have got to understand this." She was putting me under immense pressure. Finally she stared accusingly at me and said "<u>You are my mother and you are not holding me</u>."

At this point there seemed to be <u>no remaining contact with me</u> as analyst.

I think the reader can see from these quotes that in the enacted dimension of the treatment, the patient was reliving her experience of herself and her mother during the barrier nursing: she felt small, vulnerable, and prevented from getting the food/nourishment she needed, even though it was right there in front of her; she was dying inside and barely holding on to life, even though the helicopter/mother, albeit at a distance, was holding onto her; she experienced the barrier nursing concretely and physically as a sheet of glass, like a car windshield, and there were no wipers to dry her tears in the terrible storm; she alternated between worrying and fearing that her analyst/mother could not bear the suffering they were both going through, and berating her analyst/mother for not simply holding her baby as any mother would do.

It was at this point in the clinical sequence that Casement, as I described above, became able to effectively address his patient – from *within* the "original creation" transference–countertransference process – and address her agony from within his own experience of their ordeal together:

> You are making me experience in myself the sense of despair, and the impossibility of going on, that you are feeling. I am aware of being in what feels to me like a total paradox. In one sense I am feeling that it is impossible to reach you just now, and yet in another sense I feel that my telling you this may be the only way I can reach you . . . Similarly I feel as if it could be impossible to go on, and yet I feel that the only way I can help you through this is by my being prepared to tolerate what you are making me feel, and going on.
>
> (Casement, 1982, p. 283)

54

From within the barrier nursing trauma that was being relived by both participants in the enacted dimension of the treatment, Casement's intervention reached (touched) both the patient's infantile experience of impending psychic annihilation (Hurvich, 1989, 2004) as well as her higher-level ego capacities, thus setting the stage for her to be able to bring her more mature self to bear on her traumatic infantile experience. Returning to the original clinical sequence:

> After a long silence Mrs. B began to speak to me again as analyst. She said "For the first time I can believe you, that you are in touch with what I have been feeling, and what is so amazing is that you can bear it." I was then able to interpret to her that her desperate wish for me to let her touch me had been her way of letting me know that she needed me to be really in touch with what she was going through. This time she could agree. She remained in silence for the last ten minutes of this session, and I sensed that it was important that I should do nothing to interrupt this in any way.
>
> The following day Mrs. B told me what had been happening during that silence. She had been able to smell her mother's presence, and she had felt her mother's hands again holding hers. She felt that it was her mother from before the fainting [GK: and from before the barrier nursing] that she had got in touch with, as she had never felt held like that since then.

In the last session of that week,

> Mrs. B had woken feeling happy and had later found herself singing extracts from the Opera "Der Freischütz," the plot of which (she explained) includes the triumph of light over darkness. She had also dreamed that *she was in a car which had got out of control having taken on a life of its own. The car crashed into a barrier which had prevented her from running into the on-coming traffic. The barrier had saved her because it had remained firm. If it had collapsed she would have been killed.* She showed great relief that I had withstood her angry demands. My remaining firm had been able to stop the process which had taken on a life of its own, during which she had felt completely out of control. The same dream ended with *the patient reaching out to safety through the car windscreen which had opened to her like two glass doors.*

In his 2000 article, Casement states that he now realizes that his not agreeing to hold her hand had given Mrs. B a chance to refind the mother who had helped to save her life. In her mind, previous to this, her mother had always seemed to have been cruel by not being there for her when she had been most needed, at the time of the accident and later with the surgeon and, without conscious awareness of it, during the psychotic-making lack of physical/emotional contact with her mother throughout the period of barrier nursing. As she later discovered, however, her mother had in fact managed to be there in the barrier nursing despite the appearance of not being. I would add that she discovered this by reliving it in the treatment's enacted dimension, where she learned that her mother/analyst actually did care and was in contact all along.

In both papers, Casement makes the point that I have made in several places in this book: that just being a new object is not enough. A patient needs a new experience with the old object. In the first paper he quotes Winnicott (1963) in this regard:

> In the end the patient uses the analyst's failures, often quite small ones, perhaps manoeuvred by the patient . . . and we have to put up with being in a limited context misunderstood. The operative factor is that the patient now hates the analyst for the failure that originally came as an environmental factor, outside the infant's area of omnipotent control, but that is now staged in the transference. So in the end we succeed by failing – failing the patient's way. This is a long distance from the simple theory of cure by corrective experience.
>
> (Casement, 1982, p. 258)

In the second paper, he puts it this way:

> This is where the patient needed to be able to experience her old self, apparently with old other (thought to have withdrawn like mother), beyond which she could discover a new other who could – after all – survive the intensity of her feelings about that withdrawal. In working through that new experience (with me as the surviving, and therefore new, other) Mrs. B could then begin to experience herself as new self with new other.
>
> (Casement, 2000, p. 175, footnote)

Note

1 As I have already noted, I believe the concept of interactive enacted processes has more explanatory power than the concept of projective identification, because it conceptualizes the unintended contribution of the analyst's unconscious dynamics to the analytic process and its therapeutic outcome.

7

INTERACTION IN PSYCHOANALYSIS

Across and Through the Interpsychic "Cat-Flap"

All contemporary psychoanalytic schools formally address, and in their day-to-day clinical work all practicing clinicians consider, the interactive aspects of analytic process. However, as I indicated in Chapter 3, how "interaction" is defined is another matter. In this chapter I would like to further explicate the concept of *interpsychic* interaction – the unconscious and preconscious transference–countertransference processes that underlie the enacted dimension of analytic process. I will distinguish interpsychic interaction from *interpersonal* interaction and from the concept and theory of *intersubjectivity,* and discuss how it relates to the *analytic third.* Following this theoretical grounding, I will take up the idea of *co-creation,* or *co-construction,* a term widely employed in contemporary discourse, and how it relates to what transpires in the enacted dimension. Does characterizing enactment as "co-created" or "co-constructed" clarify or obscure the nature of the unconscious, dynamic process involved? What exactly is it that is co-created?

Interpsychic Interaction and Interpersonal Interaction

"Interaction" is a broad everyday term but is not in itself a psychoanalytic concept. It encompasses all forms of communication – conscious and unconscious, verbal and nonverbal – between any two people. "Interpsychic interaction" is a specific psychoanalytic concept; it refers to *unconscious* transference–countertransference communication – the unconscious resonances and interpenetrations that take place when the psyches of patient and analyst meet in analytic space. It is in this realm or subset of patient–analyst interaction that the enacted dimension of analytic process evolves.

"Interpersonal interaction" is also a broad everyday term that may refer to any form of communication/interaction between two people and is not, unless further defined as such, a psychoanalytic concept. When the term is used in a psychoanalytic context, its meaning is not necessarily the same as what I have been describing as interpsychic interaction. Depending on the particular theorist, interpersonal interaction may refer to anything along the continuum from interpsychic interaction at one end, to interaction in its very broad, general sense at the other.

The distinction I am making between everyday terms and psychoanalytic concepts applies as well to "action" and "enactment." Action is not a psychoanalytic concept; enactment, is. Sandler's passing the tissue box to his patient, all would agree, was an action. Just about anything that occurs in the consulting room is an action – walking into the office, lying on the couch, talking or not talking, interpreting or remaining silent. What makes an action like Sandler's passing the tissue box also an enactment is the fact that it actualized – made psychically real in the analytic engagement – unconscious wishes, defenses, and compromise formations in both the patient and analyst. Enactment – that is, the enacted dimension of analytic process – evolves out of the unconscious *interpsychic* interaction between the analytic dyad.

Bolognini's (2011) metaphor of a "cat-flap" provides a rich, visual depiction of the interpsychic realm and how it differs both from intrapsychic experience and from interpersonal interaction (as well from other forms of unconscious projective/introjective interactions which he terms "transpsychic"). A cat-flap is the swinging flap at the bottom of an entry door to a house through which the house cat can come and go unheeded, unseen, and without disturbing its owners, intent on other pursuits:

> In my opinion, it is a good symbol for a structural (it is part of the door) and functional (it was specifically designed to so that the cat can carry out its function of catching mice inside and outside the house) device that is not only intrapsychic but also interpsychic. The cat-flap is quite distinct from the door, which allows the passage of people, and from incidental cracks, which allow the passage of mice, clandestine, parasitical guests that harm the community/interpsychic–relational apparatus.
>
> I conjecture that the cat-flap device corresponds topically to a preconscious mental level, and relationally to an interpsychic level; it does not imply a total and "official" (interpersonal) opening of the door, and at the same time it does not correspond to the unconscious cracks and "transpsychic" transmission levels on which the "mice"/projective pathological identifications carry out their actions. Analysis "constructs a cat-flap" and coaches the "cat" (the preconscious) to use it.
>
> In the interpsychic exchange, with a saving of energy, we often implicitly – but also instinctively and consensually – accept that the "cat" comes in and goes out, that it goes back and forth between us and the others. At times we see and notice it; at others

we do not. Its passing is a natural, noninvasive, and nonparasitical event that is not subject to rigid control and that generally does not disturb us.

(Bolognini 2011, p. 67)

The concept of interpsychic interaction – as an unambiguous *psychoanalytic concept* – provides the clearest way to describe what is essential about enactment and enactive processes. It focuses psychoanalytic attention on the transference and countertransference actualizations that are continuously evolving at this *preconscious/unconscious* level of patient–analyst interaction rather than on the overt, behavioral/interpersonal manifestations of that process, thereby avoiding many of the definitional problems reviewed in Chapter 3, as well as clarifying that enacted processes are not in the realm of conscious analytic technique. (The relationship of the enacted dimension to analytic technique is taken up more fully in the next chapter.)

Interpsychic Interaction and Intersubjectivity

Many use the term intersubjectivity to describe this realm of interpsychic communication. The two concepts, however, are not identical. The term intersubjectivity is found in a variety of disciplines (philosophy, psychology, psychoanalysis, sociology, and anthropology), and is defined differently not only across disciplines but also by writers within the same discipline. In the psychoanalytic literature, writers do not always make clear whether they are referring to the conscious aspects of this interaction, its unconscious aspects, or both. Further, psychoanalytic use of the concept is often based on some form of constructivist or perspectivist epistemology which emphasizes the symmetricality and equality of interactive influence between the members of the analytic dyad, as well as the capacity of each to appreciate the separate subjectivity of the other. For some writers in this perspective, intersubjectivity, and intersubjective interaction, indeed refers to the developmental achievement of the capacity to recognize the other as a separate subjectivity (e.g., Benjamin, 1988, 1990, 1992, 2010). Other writers, whether they address this issue or not, use the terms primarily to refer to the process of reciprocal influence and regulation (a process that may be occurring on either conscious or unconscious levels) between the two parties in the dyad (e.g., Stolorow, et al., 1978, Stolorow & Atwood, 1992). Addressing these definitional differences under the rubric of "mutuality" in psychoanalysis, Aron (1996) refers to the two different usages as the "mutuality of recognition" and the "mutuality of regulation," and stresses (see also Teicholz, 1990) that analyst–patient interactions, like mother–child interactions, entail constant reciprocal regulation, but not necessarily constant reciprocal recognition.

The concept of interpsychic interaction, as I noted in Chapter 3, is rooted in an intrapsychic theory of mind which places its emphasis on the separate, primarily *unconscious,* experience of each psychic organization. As such, interpsychic interaction does not presuppose the same kind of symmetricality and mutuality of recognition in the analytic dyad, and thus encompasses not only the intersubjective experiences of comparatively more autonomous, highly organized psychic fields, but also the unconscious, "presubjective" (Bolognini, 2011) experiences found in more primitive interactional fields, those in which the more structured and developed experiences of self and other are not in the foreground. Such experiences are not only central in the treatment process of patients whose level of psychic development does not allow for the existence of a separate other, but are central as well in *all* treatment processes during periods when regressive influences may bring one or the other party to this level of psychic functioning.

More important, regardless of which may occupy the foreground, presubjective and intersubjective fields exist simultaneously. Over 40 years ago, Loewald (1970, 1979) described the two levels of interpsychic relatedness as follows:

> There are kinds of relatedness between what conventionally we refer to as self and object, which call into question the universal validity of these very terms. We have come to see that there are levels of mental functioning and experience where these distinctions are not made, or made only fleetingly and in rudimentary form. These are deep unconscious layers showing modes of interpsychic relatedness, of emotional ties that are active under the surface in both analysand and analyst, and thus in their relatedness, forming ingredients of the therapeutic potential.
>
> (Loewald 1979, p. 159)

> The psychoanalytic situation, in this regard, represents a novel interpsychic field in which more fully developed features of psychic fields, object relations, merge with or are strongly influenced by coexisting primitive features.
>
> (Loewald 1970, pp. 52–53)

Bolognini (2011), more recently, addressed this issue as well, summarizing the distinctions between interpsychic, intersubjective, and interpersonal interaction as follows:

> interaction is the phenomenological common denominator among these three concepts, but the interpsychic is a more extended

psychic dimension compared to the other two. The interpsychic is a level of "wide-band" functioning, in that it allows the natural, uninterrupted, and not dissociated coexistence of mental states in which the object is recognized in its separateness, alongside others in which this recognition is less clear. This does not occur for pathological reasons but is due to a temporary and transitory condition of companionable, cooperative fusion . . . which is part of the normal, good mental cohabiting of human beings.

In this sense, the image of the cat-flap is once again useful, symbolizing something different and intermediate between the opening of the "interpersonal" door and the clandestine breaking-in of the "transpsychic" cracks exploited by the mice.

The interpsychic is a universal, ubiquitous dimension, but it does not presuppose that in that moment only the functional level belonging to separate subjects capable of recognizing others is working, even if it is clear that this level must have been achieved by the subject, as an advanced point of its general psychic development.

(Bolognini, 2011, p. 69)

Thus, interpsychic interaction is both a more focused concept than inter-subjective interaction in that it specifically refers to a preconscious/unconscious process, as well as a broader concept in that it includes both presubjective and more highly structured fields of relatedness. Downey (1994) has compared Loewald's "interpsychic" realm to Winnicott's "transitional" realm, as both depict a "special psychological space which individuals may enter, share, or emerge from depending upon their developmental level. It is a place where as a part of a developmental or analytic dyad they share, create, organise and differentiate in the context of their common yet separate experience" (Downey, 1994, p. 842). Bollas (2001) has referred to unconscious interpsychic interaction as "Freudian intersubjectivity," and considers the involvement of the analytic pair in this level of unconscious communication to be the hallmark of Freudian psychoanalysis.

Interpsychic Interaction, the Analytic Third, and the Enacted Dimension

The concept of the "analytic third" is intimately related to the enacted dimension of analytic process. Like "intersubjectivity," however, the concept of the third is used in different ways and has no single, agreed upon definition. In the January 2004 issue of the *Psychoanalytic Quarterly* nine prominent theorists each contributed a paper on the analytic third which resulted in at least as many definitions.

Most commonly, the third is defined within an intersubjective framework: the co-creation of a new patient–analyst subjectivity that is the central focus of analytic investigation (Ogden, 1994a). As I discussed above, however, the concept of intersubjectivity does not necessarily refer specifically to the unconscious aspects of analytic interaction, nor does it necessarily encompass the presubjective interactive field that is also a continuous part of the analytic relationship. Additionally, like the problem with the word "enactment" (discussed in Chapter 3), the words "the third" (as opposed to the *concept* of "the third") connote a concrete or discrete entity rather than emphasizing what is an ongoing, largely preconscious and unconscious, process.

The analytic third belongs to the interpsychic realm. I think of the third as the ongoing *process* of *interpsychic* communication – the process out of which evolves the enacted dimension of analytic treatment. In the enacted dimension, an unconscious process in the patient and an unconscious process in the analyst – the analytic "first" and the analytic "second" – interpenetrate across and through the interpsychic "cat-flap" creating a third process that partakes of, but is different from, each of these. From a contemporary Freudian *interpsychic* perspective, the essential data of analytic treatment is the process within the analytic first, the patient – the evolution of his or her unique experience and internal world – rather than, as generally emphasized in an intersubjective perspective, the third itself (or the contribution made to it by the analytic second, the analyst), which is considered only one of several routes, albeit an important route, to the essential data. This brings us to the question of what is actually meant by the concept of "co-creation."

Co-Creation

So what exactly is "co-created" in an enacted process? Looking back at the three vignettes presented in Chapters 5 and 6, clearly both patient and analyst are involved in each enacted process described. But to what aspect of this process should we apply the term "co-creation"? Is it accurate to say, as some social-constructivist and intersubjective theoretical perspectives do, that the patient's transference, and/or the analyst's countertransference, are "co-created"? From the interpsychic perspective that underlies my conception of the enacted dimension of analytic process, I would make the following distinction: it is only the particular *form* taken by the unconscious transference–countertransference interpenetration that is co-created and as such unique to each particular patient–analyst dyad. (In the Sandler vignette, the passing, and the not passing, of the tissue box; in the Renik vignette, the two-year period of mutual idealization; and in the Casement vignette, the interactions around the question of hand-holding.)

However, the patient's transference and analyst's countertransference themselves are not co-created. Each is a unique, separate entity, each the product of a unique psychic organization (see also Chused, 1991; Smith, 1993). In all three vignettes, patient and analyst each had a different unconscious motivation, based on a different genetic history, for becoming involved in the enacted process, and each had their own separate unconscious experience of what they were co-creating. Their separate issues were congruent enough, however, that patient and analyst could unconsciously co-create an analytic experience that actualized both. In effect, two separate intrapsychic dramas blended to look like one interpersonal play (see Chused, in Chused et al., 1999).

Let me take this distinction – between the co-created part of an enactment and the underlying psychic processes – a bit further. As a product of the mind (in this case, two minds), an enacted process can be usefully likened to a dream (in this case, a two-party, waking dream [see Kern, 1987]). The observable, action component of an enactment is equivalent to a dream's manifest content; the unconscious wishes, defenses, or early object relationship that the action actualizes are equivalent to a dream's latent meaning. Dreams use sensory images as the vehicle to provide the unconscious wishes with disguised, but experientially "real," expression; enacted processes use action (both motor action and verbal action) to provide the interpenetration of unconscious transference and countertransference fantasies with disguised, but experientially "real," expression. In other words, enactments have the same psychic structure and function as any other psychic phenomenon or product of the mind. Dreams, fantasies, symptoms, and enactments are all complex, overdetermined compromise formations that serve expressive, defensive, and adaptive functions.

Keeping in mind the analogy to dreams, and remembering the distinction between the manifest and latent components of an enacted process, enables us to be clearer about what is, and what is not, unconsciously co-created in an enacted process, and it also helps us understand the relationship between enactment and analytic technique, which is the subject of the next chapter.

8

ENACTMENT AND ANALYTIC TECHNIQUE

What We Can Learn from John Lennon and Microwave Ovens

In this chapter I will address the following questions: How does our increased awareness of the enacted dimension of analytic process affect how we conduct analytic treatment? Do we need to alter our technical principles? Have they even, as some have suggested, become obsolete and expendable? As I noted in Chapter 3, the different ways in which theorists understand and define enactment, as well as the different ways in which theorists conceptualize what we mean by patient–analyst interaction (discussed in the last chapter), lead to different answers to these questions. Definitions that emphasize the interpersonal or behavioral aspects of enactment, particularly when they are in the context of an analytic theory that stresses the contributions of the analyst's subjectivity and favors a more active and interactive analytic stance, tend to view enactment in the context of analytic technique. The concept of the enacted dimension, which emphasizes the underlying unconscious interpsychic process of the phenomenon, views "enactment" as outside the domain of explicit technical interventions and as furthering our understanding, not of technique, but of the therapeutic action of psychoanalysis.

Owen Renik (1993b, 1999, 2007) has been a particularly active proponent of the idea that the analyst's "irreducible subjectivity" and the intersubjective nature of the clinical encounter necessitate revisions in how we conduct analytic treatment. For example, he suggests that "we discard a widely held principle of technique, which holds that countertransference enactment ... is to be avoided" (1993b, p. 562). He cites the vignette he presented in his earlier paper (Renik, 1993a, and described in this volume in Chapter 5, "The Hostile Interpretation") as an illustration of how "acting unselfconsciously on a wish to compete with and punish a patient was the basis for a very effective analytic intervention," adding that "sometimes it is useful for an analyst to accept the need to act under the influence of personal motivations *of which he or she has become aware* before those motivations can be thoroughly investigated" (Renik, 1993a, p. 563; emphasis added). This suggestion that there be a role for "countertransference enactment" in conscious analytic technique is misguided for a number of reasons. First, Renik's hostile interpretation was not a considered technical decision; it was part and parcel of a two-year *unconscious* enacted process. The timing of its occurrence was influenced by factors that were beyond his control and outside the province of conscious technique. Second, Renik was not simply expressing "personal motivations" about which he had "become aware," he was involuntarily expressing *particular* personal motivations that were stimulated by the patient's enacted transference process, with which they joined in an unconscious, interpsychic process. Third, the therapeutic recreation of the patient's trauma and the ways it organized his internal object-relational patterns was not, as he suggests, *initiated* by the hostile interpretation. The recreation had been unconsciously evolving in the treatment's enacted dimension over its entire two years. The hostile interpretation was the *endpoint* of its first phase. It was a turning point that signified that an analytic transformation had already occurred. The patient had become ready, and had perhaps unconsciously communicated this to the analyst, to reexperience his infantile trauma, allowing the two dimensions of the transference to be productively integrated. While Renik's action did facilitate the analytic process, it did not do so through a change in technique.

Simply put, enactments are not technical procedures. Technique is what we consciously, intentionally strive to do; an enactment is an *unconscious* transference–countertransference *process*. To put it another way, enactments are a *de*scriptive part of analytic process, not a *pre*scriptive component of analytic technique. And here I come to John Lennon. What does the late Beatles songwriter and singer have to say about enactments and their relationship to technique and analytic process? There's a line in one of his songs (the song is "Beautiful Boy" and it is on the *Double Fantasy* album, 1980) that goes, "Life is what happens to you while you're busy making other plans." To paraphrase: enactments are what happen to you while you are doing psychoanalysis. Enactments will occur, without awareness or intent, regardless of what you think you are doing or are intending to do, regardless of the analytic theory you profess, regardless of whether you are scrupulous or free-wheeling in your approach to technique. No analytic practitioner is immune. You will become aware that an enacted process has occurred in retrospect, generally at a dynamically meaningful juncture in the treatment. (In the Sandler vignette, at the symbolically significant two-and-a-half year marker; in the Renik vignette, at the symbolically significant two-year marker.) It is only then, after the underlying unconscious transference–countertransference process becomes conscious, that one's analytic technique, however conceived, is deployed to analyze the enacted process just as one would do with any other psychic phenomenon that presented itself.

The idea that enactments are what happen to us while we are doing psychoanalysis is also illustrated in the Casement vignette. In his discussion of this vignette in the original paper Casement speculates on his technical handling of the abstinence principle:

> It is a matter for speculation whether I would have been so fully subjected to the necessary impact of this patient's experience had I not first approached the question of possible physical contact as an open issue. Had I gone by the book, following the classical rule of no physical contact under any circumstance, I would certainly have been taking the safer course for me but I would probably then have been accurately perceived by the patient as actually afraid even to consider such contact. I am not sure that the reliving of this early trauma would have been as real as it was to the patient, or in the end so therapeutically effective, if I had been preserving myself throughout at that safer distance of classical "correctness." Instead I acted upon my intuition of the moment, and it is uncanny how precisely and unwittingly this led me to reenact with the patient this detail of the original trauma, which she needed to be able to experience within the analytic relationship and to be genuinely angry about.
>
> (Casement, 1982, p. 284)

Casement's speculations about his technical decisions miss an important point: while another analyst might have had a choice, *he* did not. Casement's sense of the "uncanny" speaks to the fact that his technical decisions were being co-opted by unconscious enacted processes. His conscious "decision" to hold the question of hand-holding in abeyance, as well as the timing of his conveying to the patient his reconsidered "decision" not to hold her hand, were each an unconscious compromise formation, fashioned out of the patient's pressure toward transference actualization and the press toward actualization of the analyst's own interpenetrating countertransference, tempered by his work ego and analytic conscience. *These "intuitive" decisions were each the only decision this particular analyst could make with this particular patient at those particular moments.* Thus it was not really "uncanny" how precisely and unwittingly Casement reenacted with the patient the original trauma. This is precisely what occurs in the enacted dimension of analytic process, and how it may be creatively utilized by a sensitive and capable clinician.

At the same time, it is important to note that despite the way in which Casement's technical decisions about abstinence became enlisted in the service of enacted processes (see Jacobs, 1986), abstinence remained an established *principle* within Casement's work ego. This principle served him as the yardstick against which to assess his ongoing conduct of the treatment, ultimately enabling him to recognize the enacted transference process and to identify his enacted over-identification with the patient that had compromised his capacity to resolve the crisis. The same is true in the Renik vignette: the principle, or value, of analytic restraint enabled Renik to recognize his atypical comment and to attend more carefully to what was occurring in himself and in the transference–countertransference matrix.

Thus, John Lennon notwithstanding, there is a particular sense in which enactment does have a relationship to analytic technique: it is in the relationship it bears to the analytic frame. Setting up and maintaining an *analytic* frame (as opposed to, for instance, a behavior therapy frame) is what creates the space for these unplanned enacted processes to occur, and ultimately to be explored. And this brings me to microwave ovens. (I owe this metaphor for the unique way analysis works to Irving Steingart [2009].) Behavioral or cognitive treatments, Steingart pointed out, try to foster change and growth the way a conventional oven cooks food – from the outside-in, via direction and instruction. In contrast, analytic treatment fosters change and growth the way a microwave oven cooks food – from the inside-out, by unsettling entrenched internal structures and setting in motion new or previously frozen psychological processes. I would extend this metaphor to highlight the relationship between the analytic frame and enacted processes as follows. The analytic frame provides the potential space (the oven) for the mixture of inchoate transference and countertransference fantasies to germinate and ultimately actualize each other in an enacted process. Within the structure and safety of the analytic frame, this transference–countertransference mixture "cooks" (to continue the metaphor), that is, it gradually becomes fully actualized: the patient comes to have the unconscious experience of living through a new treatment version of an early trauma or significant early object-relationship. At the same time, the unique structure, function, and safety of the frame also ensures that the analyst will become a new therapeutic object providing the opportunity for this new edition of the trauma to take a different path.

To put the relationship between the frame and enacted processes in nonculinary terms: each concept derives its analytic meaning with reference to the other; they are dialectically related. An enactment is an *unintended, but dynamically meaningful, departure* from the optimal analytic attitude that the frame is intended to promote. Without that analytic context, an enactment is simply a real-life interpersonal event. And with the understanding that transference–countertransference intertwinings in the enacted dimension of the treatment are evolving continuously, we can conceptualize the technical components of the frame with reference to them. As Loewald puts it with regard to analytic neutrality: "neutrality constitutes a resting point or mean around which ... [transference–countertransference] dynamics oscillate with greater or smaller amplitude" (1986, p. 281). In this conceptualization, neutrality is not an a-priori rule or a procedure; it is the place we are always in the process of reaching, the touchstone by which we come to be able to recognize that an enacted process has been occurring.[1] So, while it is true that the analyst's subjectivity makes ideal technique unattainable, and ensures the inevitability of enacted processes, the analyst's subjectivity does not render the technical principles that constitute the frame obsolete or expendable. Without them, enactment has no *analytic* meaning.

The Expansion of Analytic Data, Analytic Sensibility, and the Analytic Attitude

Having taken pains to differentiate the unconscious nature of enacted processes and their independence from any conscious technical approach, I would also point out that, as with any advance in our understanding of clinical process or the therapeutic action of psychoanalysis, awareness of the existence of the enacted dimension of the treatment will affect how we listen and to what we attend. While such expanded awareness will not make us immune from our continuous involvement in enacted processes, it does increase the array of data potentially available for analytic investigation – the not-yet-conscious world of actualizations that are continuously being created and communicated, through verbal and nonverbal action, by both patient and analyst. Further, the analyst's awareness of the inevitability and ubiquity of his or her own unwitting participation in enacted processes can help moderate concern, self-criticism, and shame (see also Aron, 2003; Chused, 2003; S. J. Ellman, 1998) regarding lapses in technique and intrusions of countertransference, allowing the analyst to include these as well in the data to be investigated, and to consider how they may be forming an essential and facilitating part of the analytic process.

Thus, awareness of the inevitability and centrality of the enacted dimension broadens what Schafer (1983) called "the analytic attitude." Such expansion of how the analyst thinks about the analytic data, and about the fact that he or she will inevitably, unconsciously, be playing a role in "the play within the play," can help sustain a treatment when little seems to be going on, or when "resistance" seems to be overwhelming. In cases of dramatic and even disruptive behavior (see, for example, the case of Jimmy in Chapter 12), this can fortify the analytic patience needed to treat the behavior as a necessary and integral part of the treatment and to tolerate not being able to fully understand it or usefully interpret it for long periods of time. The analyst can always be assured that, in any treatment, significant developments are continuously taking place, outside of awareness, in the enacted dimension of the treatment.

Each theoretical orientation, and each practicing clinician, values a different conscious technical approach: some emphasize subjective involvement in the process while others emphasize a more objective assessment; some proceed from a "one-person" perspective, others from a "two-person" perspective; some value interpretive functioning and the provision of insight and understanding, while others value experiential functioning via modeling and mentalizing for the patient. Regardless of one's particular conscious technical approach, it is the capacity to flexibly and continually oscillate among all of these that differentiates free-floating responsiveness of an analytic kind from the spontaneous responses of everyday life. Working together, as Jacobs (1997) notes, these elements create the mix of insight, expressiveness, and restraint that is essential for effective analytic work to take place. Most important, it is this feature of the analyst's mind at work that provides the analytic space for the enacted dimension of analytic process to evolve, and puts the analyst and patient in the best position to ultimately recognize it and use it in the service of promoting therapeutic change.

Note

1 More recently, Gerson (1996, p. 630) expressed this idea as follows: "Neutrality comes into existence only as the analyst and patient emerge from their embeddedness in a particular aspect of the transference–countertransference."

9

ENACTMENT AND ACTUALIZATION IN A 13-YEAR TREATMENT

The following case presentation by Katherine Oram provides us not only with a sensitive description of a 13-year analysis but also with detailed clinical process that is richly annotated with the analyst's own thoughts and reactions as the session unfolded. My discussion describes how overt "enactments" around session frequency, hand-holding, and countertransference expressions of anger are more usefully understood as actualizations of important developmental events and internalized object relationships being reexperienced in the enacted dimension of the treatment.

Arthur[1]

Introduction

Arthur is a thin, attractive man in his early 50s. He keeps himself in excellent physical shape and recently has started to cut his hair very close so as to disguise his balding. He is a man who lives by routines. He usually arrives promptly for his appointment, sets his briefcase down on my chair, takes his shoes off and lies down on my couch. At the end of the session he sits up and while he is putting his shoes back on he continues to talk often in a more spontaneous and related manner than during the session.

He is in the 14th year of an analysis that started in the summer of 1995. The first two years he came four times a week. He then moved to three times a week and starting this September (2008) he has been coming once a week (more about this later). He uses the couch although there was a period around six years ago when he sat up. This lasted for a few months and then he chose to lie down again. He is aware that the choice to lie down or sit up is his. When I initially began seeing him he worked in a small film company. He left that partnership and started his own company which survived in a marginal way for a number of years. During this time he not

71

only tried to get normal projects for his company but he also had some projects that were extremely creative and idiosyncratic in their conception that he was passionate about. There was always an undercurrent in the treatment about whether I (and other people) would see them as impossible dreams. This was always contrasted with his determination to make them into a reality. About a year and a half ago, around the time of the death of his father, his company took off and in addition, one of these projects became a reality. At present he is struggling with these successes and the various psychological issues that they have raised for him.

He is someone who does have long-standing male friends. Over the course of the analysis he discarded some of his friends who seemed more abusively competitive and developed friendships with men who seem more supportive.

Presenting Problem

Arthur's first session was on the anniversary of his mother's death. She had died suddenly of heart failure when he was in his mid-twenties. In this first session he told me that he wanted to be able to cry. As you will see his ability to feel is a central issue. He also said that he was 40 years old and had never had sexual intercourse. His relationships with women were always sexual and he enjoyed sex but he was convinced that if he tried to have intercourse he would not succeed. There was a physical problem which he described as having to do with the musculature and the way his penis was attached to his body. Because of this his erections would not stand up and he had to hold his penis with his hand. He was convinced that if he tried to enter a woman that his penis would not be able to penetrate because of this problem. Throughout the first part of the treatment the idea that this was a physical problem dominated. He went to a variety of doctors who talked to him about various surgical procedures they could do to handle this difficulty but it remained ambiguous for him (and for me) how much was physical and how much was psychological. He never chose to have any of these procedures. It was also clear that although he had had a series of short-term relationships with women none of them had been particularly intimate. It was not clear to me if this was something that he wanted.

Family History

Family structure: Arthur is the middle child of three. There is an older brother and a younger sister. His father was a dentist; his mother a teacher. Though they were a liberal Jewish family they moved to a conservative and non-Jewish town in New Jersey when Arthur was 13.

Arthur's older brother was described as a difficult, physically aggressive boy who had a problematic relationship with their mother. He was often physically aggressive with Arthur. One way Arthur handled this was by shifting his brother's focus to the tormenting of their younger sister. This mode of dealing with other males' aggression has continued in the way he uses stories of his exploits with women to entertain his male friends. Arthur describes his father, who died two and a half years ago, as a distant and critical man whose life revolved around his work. He is described as an obsessional man who frustrated his wife with his unadventurous and fearful disposition.

A central memory of Arthur's relationship to his father has to do with having just learned to drive. He was backing the car out of the garage and his father reacted as if he were about to have an accident even though there was no problem with his driving. This was representative of Arthur's feeling that his father could never validate him as a competent and independent male. When Arthur first began the analysis he still used his father as his dentist. It was totally ego-syntonic for the two of them to have his father do fillings and root canals. He stopped using his father as his dentist a year or so into the treatment. Arthur's mother was described as the center of the family, adored by both Arthur and his father. She was seen as a creative, socially conscious, woman who was frustrated in her ability to fully develop herself. She looked to Arthur to be the one who would fulfill her dreams since the older brother had distanced himself from her. Arthur describes himself as a rather shy, dreamy child, small for his age, who would spend hours building sandcastles by himself. There are descriptions of his mother's frustrated reaction to Arthur's intense separation anxiety. He was to be different than the rest of the family, a person who could move out into the world in an independent and active way.

A central memory in relation to his mother takes place in his early adolescence. He described his mother's frustration when he refused to go up on a stage to audition for a play. Compounding his early history of timidity was his slow physical development and a late puberty (I believe at 15 or 16 years of age). His descriptions make him sound like the skinny kid who gets sand kicked in his face by the bullies. His parents became so anxious about his not reaching puberty that they consulted doctors when he was an early adolescent thinking that he might need some growth hormones. He has no memory of either his mother or father having a reaction to the way his penis was attached to his body.

Arthur's adolescence was further complicated by his family having moved into a predominantly non-Jewish community in New Jersey when he was an adolescent. He has described the difficulty he had as a shy,

73

late-to-mature, Jewish adolescent boy trying to fit into this predominantly non-Jewish community. He has also described his father's irritation with his one friend being one of the few Jewish boys in the community. His father wanted to know why he wasn't friends with the "popular" kids, and there was little recognition on the part of the parents that their son who had been brought up in a progressive, liberal Jewish family might have some difficulties in this conservative, non-Jewish community.

His later adolescence and his young adulthood became the period of his life in which he was able, at least on the surface, to become the person that his mother had wanted him to be. After graduating from college, he spent a considerable amount of time traveling and living the "adventurous" life that his mother admired and always wanted him to live.

Treatment History

Arthur had had two previous treatments: one with a behaviorist who attempted unsuccessfully to help him with his sexual difficulties and the second with an analyst who made in-depth interpretations in an attempt to touch him emotionally. Neither was successful.

My initial approach was based on my sense of Arthur as someone in whom intense anxiety around his sense of self dominated. I recognized that his sexual symptoms involved problems with aggression, intense separation anxiety, and strong passive homosexual wishes with resulting castration anxiety but I felt that his fear of losing himself in the other person dominated things at this time in the treatment. The intensity of his fear of losing himself could be seen in his fear of losing sight of his penis if he entered the woman's vagina.

He enjoyed oral sex and especially enjoyed being able to lie on his back while he and the woman both looked at his penis before she brought him off. I often thought that this favorite position was paralleled in the analysis with his lying on his back while we looked at his dreams together. There was also a similar fear of losing himself in the analysis. As you will hear, his difficulty in truly experiencing his life and instead his always being the observer of his life was a central issue for him and for me in the treatment. From early on dreams about being afraid of stepping into the ocean seemed to parallel this fear of being in the experience rather than observing it. He often attempted to handle the anxiety of losing himself by taking frequent "vacations" from the treatment, moving from four times to three times a week and always making sure that he left on his vacation before I left on mine. I tended not to interpret these shifts because I felt that he needed to be able to modulate the distance according to his need. Recently, his move to once a week was of a similar nature. This time,

74

however, we have talked about the less frequent sessions being connected to an attempt to feel more in control.

His tendency in his sexual relationships with women was to feel that it was their sexual desire that he was servicing and not his. This tendency to lose touch with his desire and to experience it as the other person's has been an underlying problem in the analysis. In the transference I am often the woman (mother) who is using the analysis to service my needs, not his. Thus transference interpretations have, up until recently, been experienced as my wish to be central. In addition, his being able to feel, though he desperately desires this himself, becomes something in the transference that I want from him to make me feel good about myself. Although over the last few years I have been more able to interpret the transference directly, in the beginning of the analysis I focused on these issues in his outside relationships rather than in relation to me.

At the start of treatment the most conscious transference was to me as the ineffective, devalued woman. In fact, when he first called me he asked for a "low fee" analyst. I was looking for my second NYU control case and I was glad to take him on as a patient at a greatly reduced fee but I was aware of a great deal of denigration in the way he initially saw me. He was very concerned in the beginning that I was too laid back and that what he really needed was someone who could break into the emotionless state that he lived in. I was aware that this had occurred with his first analyst and they had ended up in a sado-masochistic power struggle. I could see the temptation here, and in fact had to guard against very strong countertransference feelings that had to do with wanting to prove to him that I could be of value by helping him with his sexual symptom. The more I became invested in helping him with his "symptom" the less he felt this difficulty was something of his that he was struggling with and the more he saw it as something that I needed to fix in order to make myself feel better. It became my narcissistic injury, and his experience was that he and the analysis were simply tools that I used to heal my own wound.

I think that it is important for me to note that the person that I am describing has been very well hidden until the past few years by the persona of someone who seemed like the perfect analytic patient. He was always on time, bringing in multiple dreams, and enjoying the process of analyzing himself. Spontaneous experiences quickly became stories with him being the central character that he observed. Initially, spontaneous moments were rare. They mostly occurred at the end of each session when he would sit up before leaving. All of a sudden I was able to say things to him that he was able to take in. A one-person world became a two-person world. Initially, I did not draw his attention to how different he was at the end of the sessions. I was concerned that if I did that he might respond intellectually to my inquiries but that emotionally he would shut down. I also did not suggest that he sit up for fear that he would experience it as my taking over something that he was doing on his own initiative. Over time, there has been an increase in spontaneous moments within the sessions. I remember when he first giggled in response to a humorous remark of mine. I felt like I was tickling a small child. He also began to talk about his story-telling and his sense of emotional removal.

As stated before, my approach in the beginning consisted of my allowing him to take whatever distance he needed from the analysis and not interpreting the anxiety that I thought he was trying to manage. This included his use of dreams and the way he handled the scheduling of our time around vacations. In addition, I worked very hard in order to use my countertransference as analytic information so that the understanding of his symptom remained central and the wish to resolve his symptom and the conflicts around it remained his and not mine. Not an easy task. My approach to his sexual symptom was to try to understand the conflicts underlying his anxiety as well as to support his stopping his sexual activity when he began to lose touch with his sexual desire.

Six years into the analysis (2001) he met a young woman, G, who was sufficiently distant and sufficiently uninterested in sexual intercourse to allow him the psychological space to begin to have a significantly more intimate relationship than he had ever had. She, like all of his previous interests, was not Jewish. She was blond, blue-eyed and had a slender boyish build. About a year into the relationship he was able to have sexual intercourse. However, it occurred without any physical feeling. He remained the observer.

It was striking to me that at this time he became quite depressed. In part he seemed to be responding to having to come to grips with his symptom being psychologically determined not physically determined. This meant that he had spent a good deal of his life suffering in a way that he did not have to. Two years later, the relationship broke up, in part because he began wanting more from her than she was willing or able to give and he was devastated.

His whole life became organized around the idea that his next successes, whether they were with women or in his career would undo the humiliation and devastation that had occurred with G. He has not attempted sexual intercourse since that breakup. Again, similar to his reaction to his sexual success with G, as he became more successful in his business life his upset and frustration has increased. The promise that success would cure all of his ills had not materialized. What these changes have resulted in, however, is that the over-intellectualized, flat-affected man has been replaced by an angry and disgruntled man who has been able to share with me his frustrations with the people surrounding him, including myself. In addition, I found myself becoming more and more confrontational with him about the way he insulated himself in a one-person world. This was particularly true in response to his holding on to the fantasies of his search of the perfect young woman who would be the perfect cure. Countertransferentially, I found myself frequently feeling very frustrated and contemptuous of him, and I wondered how much of my frustration and contempt was coming from some projected part of himself and how much from my own frustration.

Arthur's project was finally realized and became a success. It was at this time that his sense of disappointment and frustration intensified as well as feelings of loneliness and hopelessness. This success, which was to be the final revenge for all the hurts that he had endured and the healing of his sense of isolation, was not sufficient. I also became aware that he was angry at me because I had never gone to see it. I had not realized, and he had not said, that it was important for me to validate his achievement in the real world and not simply in his rendition of the real world in the analytic hour. This was added to a grudge that he already carried about my lack of availability when his father died while I was away on my August vacation. Furthermore, I continued to be extremely confrontational about his insistence that the world had to mirror his fantasies and that this was the only possible cure for his troubles. I now think that my countertransference was out of control and that my reaction to his projection onto me of a worthless and inadequate self had taken hold. I was as angry with him as he was with me and it made it impossible for me to understand how terrified and helpless and inadequate he felt about what a two-person relationship is all about.

In the summer of 2007 around the same time as the completion of his project he began to talk about stopping the analysis. Feelings about what more he could get from the analysis dominated. Our struggles around his magical thinking about the cure for his ills being in the external world and my view that the cure was internal were central. I also understood his thinking of leaving the treatment as his attempts to sort himself out from me. We had a peculiar arrangement in which he came up with a date at the end of December when he "might" stop. It was not until a couple of weeks before that deadline that it became clear that he was, in fact, going to stop. We continued to work on the possible understandings of this decision until the end of the final hour. I felt very touched in that final hour. He talked about feeling stuck in where he was but not knowing where to go. The old ways of magical thinking were no longer working but he did not know how to move forward. He seemed to be struggling with trying to propel himself into life by leaving the analysis in which the seduction to stay in a merged, dreamlike state with me seemed overwhelming. We parted with his saying that he would call me in a month to talk about whether and/or how to proceed.

A month later he returned for a session. He was clearly concerned that I was not going to welcome him back. He described being in a lot of pain as he grappled with where he was in the reality of his life, how odd and different he felt from the people around him, but how despite this pain he has been able to mobilize himself in his actual life in a way that he had not been able to before. I was struck by what seemed like an increased capacity to reflect on his situation and himself but also how lonely and in pain he seemed to be. He told me that he wanted to continue in this way but would probably check in with me again.

He checked in another time, and then in April he again returned, seriously depressed and rapidly became unable to function. He talked of needing to be hospitalized and imagined being in the hospital and being fed by tubes. I sent him to a psychiatrist who put him on medication. His paralysis meant that his business was teetering on the edge of failure. His friends were clearly worried about him. His depression seemed to be partly in response to a struggle with a very sadistic powerful client by whom he was feeling dominated. I also found out later that part of what had occurred when he had left the analysis is that he had reconnected with the woman, G, he had had intercourse with in the hope of rekindling their relationship and that attempt had failed. He connected his collapse to the collapse that his father had gone through when his mother had died. He had always had great contempt for his father's behavior. I was very worried about him. He was becoming less and less able to talk about what was going on. On a Monday he asked if I would hold his hand. I did. I felt that he was struggling to have contact with me but even with the holding of my hand my sense was that the predominant part of the experience was of his seeing himself holding my hand, a story that he was telling himself. I then became worried when I saw him that Thursday morning and he was comatose on my coach, eyes closed, head back, mouth open. I held his hand again. We talked about his going to the hospital but decided that he should come back and I saw him two more times that day. I then saw him on the Friday and once over the weekend. By the time I saw him on the weekend he was beginning to seem more like his normal self and beginning to be able to talk about what was happening. We continued to meet over the next few weeks and he talked about his experiencing me as a "big-hipped woman" who wanted to have intercourse with him and how repulsed he was by this.

The idea of a big black hole that was going to suck him in emerged. This soon receded and by the end of that time, within a month, he seemed to be back to his old self. He had reasserted himself in his business and he had met a young woman.

I was struggling with the dilemma of how to think about his resuming regularly scheduled appointments. I shared with him my dilemma. If I pushed for him to come back with regularly scheduled sessions he might very well feel that the sessions were something that I desired not that he desired, that they were mine not his. However, if I did not push to have him come back there was the possibility that he might feel uncared for and not wanted. He responded to my articulation of this dilemma by deciding that he would come back once a week and that if he wanted to see me more in a given week that he would let me know.

This occurred in May of 2008. I started seeing him again on a once-a-week basis. As he reconstituted himself, the devaluation of me and the process we were both engaged in intensified to proportions that I had not experienced before. He became involved with a young woman that May and began to describe his recovery as being due to her. In addition, he gave some credit to the medication although he quickly cut it down to a minimal dosage that he took only five days a week. He was scornful of the female psychiatrist who had the nerve to charge him a significant sum. I was pointedly left out as being one of the helpful parts of his recovery. In the fall of 2008 when it looked to me as if we were on a permanent once-a-week schedule I raised our renegotiating the fee. I felt that he could certainly afford my full fee since he had been paying me more than that on a weekly basis for the three sessions. He was extremely dismissive of my being justified and could not imagine paying me my full fee because it would mean that I would be making more than he charged his clients. We ended up agreeing that I would charge him a little less than my full fee because it would have meant such a huge leap in terms of what he was used to paying per session but that in six months I would raise it again.

The session that you are about to hear takes place at the end of December. As you will hear it occurs in the midst of this intense transference–countertransference muddle. He had truly gotten to me and this was no longer an affectless, intellectualized treatment. I was furious with him and my various attempts to understand what was going on in such a way that I could regain control of myself had not been particularly successful.

The December Session

Came a few minutes late. (*I was aware that coming late is not typical for him.*)

Goes into a whole thing about how he should get himself a Blackberry, panicked about being late here, had been in the midst of writing a note to his nephew, his sister's son. He had blanked out on the appointment. He is going into a whole thing about his difficulty remembering, how it's a whole "cat and mouse" game. (*I prick up my ears at the phrase "cat and mouse" game." I know that frequently he will be unaware of using phrases or words that point to something more than what is active on the surface. I am thinking to myself that a cat and mouse game usually has to do with two people. I am thinking about*

79

his being late and wondering how that fits in. I am also poised for what I now understand is my "pounce" {i.e. that I have the goods} while at the same time I am feeling frustrated at his talking about this whole incident as if it is simply between him and his memory. I am also aware in a rather irritable way that for someone who has been in analysis for many years he seems unbelievably uncurious about his lateness.)

If he gets a Blackberry then he won't take the time to get to know how it works, doesn't have interest knowing how it functions. I ask about the "cat and mouse game." To forget or not to forget, will he or won't he. He does set the alarm in his mind, but doesn't know why he would remember. *(I am thinking about cat and mouse having something to do with me, and with his "why would he remember" {the appointment}. I am beginning to feel annoyed at the idea that the appointment is not of enough value to him to remember it. I am also aware that he is acting as if the cat and mouse has simply to do with two sides of him and that there is a negation of my existence as if I do not exist.)*

He goes back to saying "What is the game?" I say, "You know it isn't that you didn't remember, you did remember but just in time to be late." He gets very defensive. Says that the cat-and-mouse game is about will he or will he not forget and how it would be a hell of a lot easier to buy a Blackberry. To not have a Blackberry is not good for his emotional state since he gets into these panics, the fear of blowing it although he didn't blow it. *(I am feeling extremely irritated.)* I say to him: "You're acting very naive as if you're not aware of how these things work, is there some way I can get you curious about why you were late?" *(I know that there is a lot of irritation in my voice.)*

He goes back to the cat-and-mouse game and starts to talk about how he feels like he is a spinning top, not blowing things like the appointment, but that the world out there is "putting demands on me, me against the world." *(I am thinking that he is talking about me in this distanced way.)*

He continues: "I come here so that you know that I remember to show up. On the way over I was anxious about being late. Why should I be so anxious? It is my time, I'm late. She'll know I'm not on top of things. I've been early mostly. It shows that I'm in control, on top of things. It's important to show that I am on top of things."

I say: "But this morning you showed me that you were not on top of things."

He responds that that's what the anxiety was about. It was about being late. "You must be getting at something else," he says to me. "Cat and mouse? I don't value you by not showing up on time?" He then goes on to say, "I don't think I've been valuing the sessions much recently because they are expensive." *(I am getting more and more irritated and I say to myself, "just sit with the irritation.")*

He continues: "They're not as integrated into my life. I do seem outside, they're not as integrated. They're ... (trails off and then continues) I wonder if there's fear left over. Better to not stop again. Remember what happened last time." (He's reporting what he says to himself). "It's not analysis any more, it's maintenance." (*I hear the "it's not analysis anymore" as "I am not going to do the analytic work anymore" and my annoyance intensifies.*) "There's a lot of things about coming. Whether I'm in or whether I'm out. I still think of it as treading water. I can't do with it, I can't do without it. The financial thing is, it's expensive."

I say: "You know you are in analysis, in fact, you're in the midst of a very intense process, only I don't know if you really want to look at what is going on."

He responds: "Yeah, hard to know what I'm interested in. Just a tremendous relief that I'm not where I was, a really strong theme these days." He then talks about his being in the position of winning unlike his friends who are struggling with this economy. He talks about how everyone else is having difficulties because of the economy but he is actually doing very well: "My life is filled with the smell of winning." He talks about feeling proud that he has gotten through such a tough time. He then moves back into a more complaining tone as he talks about his irritation with his friends. Two of them, who share his office, did not help with the party that they give in their joint office space. He ends up having to do it all. He talks about how one friend lost a job and the other is depressed. "I've survived, and then it's lonely."

"Now I'm taking a vacation, it's going to coincide with yours. (*Note: he is referring to the fact that this is one of the first times he has not left before I leave on vacation*). I'm going to St. Lucia on my own. It's a mature thing that I'm doing, but why am I going alone? I didn't ask Barbara. I'm being optimistic and social. I'm not as isolated and lonely and hopeless feeling as I was six months ago. I don't know what it means about here. I don't know if 5 milligrams of Lexapro four days a week is doing it. I have some sense of control. Why stop? Is this a good time to dig? Or should I just cruise?" (*He is referring to the analysis.*)

"I've won something, survived. It's not as hard when someone is stepping in front of me. I enjoy others' suffering now. The bloodlust to beat them out, even to the point of being really angry. I'm angry about the party, at the bunch of people who did not show up. My whole understanding of them not showing up is that they don't want to make me feel good. Talk about coming five minutes late!"

I responded: "Maybe you don't want me to feel good about all of these things that have happened to you."

He responds with a thoughtful "Hmm ... possible ... but why? They did it to me, I did it to you?"

81

I ask him: "What are your thoughts?" He's silent. I say that I think he has been very careful not to let me feel I've been of any help to him.

He says: "Yeah, I'm stingy. What's that about? It's not new. *(The not giving me any credit.)* It came up with G and my being able to have intercourse. My leaving you out of that and then it went through stages where I couldn't forgive you, I held a grudge. *(I'm thinking that he continues to hold a grudge.)* I felt let down by you, forgotten." *(He's referring to the fact that he sees me as not being there for him – his father dying and my not being there, an idea he has that I was on G's side.)*

"You *(he's referring to me)* just can't win," and he laughs spontaneously. I laugh also and say, "I'm aware of that, thanks for the interpretation."

"Why is that?" *(The tension between us has lessened to some extent and things feel looser.)*

He says: "I can't win then you can't win and if I do win, and we both laugh, you still can't win. It's not generous. I want to stay hurt. That's what it comes from. Even my win is not a win. It's an angry defiance. I had to scratch and crawl to get to where I am. I'm not sharing it with anyone. Why?"

He then goes on to describes his nephew having written a poem about him, Arthur, as being strong and proud and how he can't take his nephew's view of himself in. "I always erase the possibility that I'm important to someone." He then goes on to talk in a complaining tone about how would he know that he's important to his nephew, his nephew doesn't call. *(I'm thinking that he is returning to his complaining and moving away from the fact that he did get something from his nephew.)*

He talks about the ski trip he went on with his sister and her family and how it turned out to be actually good. He wonders why that kind of experience doesn't serve him in his daily life. He continues: "When I wake up at 5 a.m. what do I have to hold on to? It's always *(what he holds on to)* a woman's pussy, her breasts, the wonder of her body, the consumption of her body, the ecstasy, not by thinking about Georgie *(his nephew)*. That's the winning thing. It's always a conquest. I've got power over her. I want to expose her, see something that she doesn't show anyone else *(I'm thinking that that's what he does with me. I'm the only one who knows about his not having had intercourse)* Yeah, getting into her pants. Her revealing her private parts. Letting me consume her, play with her, so tied to starvation, rejection. Odd that I think about Barbara more fondly. Crossing the line there. The reason I've been upset." *(I think to myself that he had not mentioned being upset.)*

"She *(Barbara)* didn't email me back when I emailed her. I couldn't tell her that I wanted to see her. All I could say is that 'I'm free if you want to hang.' I think you are probably thinking that ultimately, I didn't want to put it on the line, the whole intercourse question, not wanting to humiliate myself in front of her." I respond that I wonder if another part of it is that if he brings all these feelings in here about having intercourse and that he might end up feeling humiliated in front of me. That I really think that he is much more humiliated by it than he is aware.

At first he says that he is not aware of that. Then adds: "You often throw me a bone. You've said that there are women who are not so interested in having intercourse. I keep thinking I wish that I could meet someone like that. In any case, that humiliation, there are issues about being in control, the spaghetti sauce, the hard nipple, I need to totally be in control. But why does that mean that this is painful? Every time I talk here it releases the pain. Unless I am missing something and there's a whole other level? Only reason I am here is that I can't fuck."

The session ends with his wondering about the idea that he feels humiliated. Is it true. I say, "Well there is some reason why you have to make sure that I don't feel that I'm of value, that I am not worth the money that you pay me." *(We end on that note. It feels good. For the first time in a long time I don't feel angry.)*

Addendum: At the beginning of the next session he tells me that he almost called me in between sessions to let me know that he liked the "intensity" and "out of control" feeling of the last session. He decided not to.

Discussion of the Case of Arthur

This is the case of a 40-year-old man, unhappily still a virgin, who did not feel in secure ownership of his penis. Full possession of his masculine self was threatened psychologically by a mother who used him to fulfill her own frustrated narcissistic needs; by a passive and interpersonally inadequate father who simultaneously criticized and painfully penetrated his body throughout his life; and by an older brother who physically attacked him. To make matters worse, he was physically slight of build, slow to sexually mature (he did not reach puberty until he was 15 or 16), and he believed that his penis was problematically attached. Entry into his teenage years was even further complicated by his family's move when he was 13, a shy, skinny boy given to daydreaming.

There is an enormous amount of rich material to comment on in this beautifully conducted treatment and beautifully written case report. I will, however, confine my comments to this evening's topic of enactment. I'll describe the historical and treatment contexts in which the overt "enactments" around session frequency, hand-holding, and countertransference expressions of anger occur, and try to show how these actions are more usefully understood as actualizations of important developmental events and internalized object relationships being reexperienced in the enacted dimension of this 13-year-long treatment.

My comments will be organized around four phases of the treatment: (1) the first six years, prior to Arthur's meeting G; (2) the next seven years till the point Arthur stops treatment; (3) the week of sessions in April, 2008; and (4) the process material from this past December.

Phase I: The First Six Years

The central transference–countertransference themes in these early years of treatment revolved around Arthur's need to maintain complete emotional control: his determination not to experience any feelings which, by definition, would be painfully humiliating. He maintained a "perfect-patient" demeanor for many years, a self-contained, one-person entity. Spontaneous affect could be expressed only fleetingly after the session ended. Any let-up in control during sessions was the equivalent of losing sight of his penis during intercourse: he feared emasculation and, on a deeper level, the loss of his entire self (an intense anxiety expressed in his dreams of being afraid to step into the ocean). He maintained tight emotional and intellectual control over his analytic experience, vigilant not to let Kate use him for what he experienced as her own narcissistic need to fix his "broken penis symptom," as his mother had earlier used him to fix *her* narcissistic injuries.

Kate was quite aware of what lay beneath Arthur's perfect-patient demeanor. She was aware of his subtle denigrations, his need to devalue her as an ineffective, self-interested, mother. But Kate was also aware of the potential for the transference–countertransference to devolve into an unproductive sado-masochistic power struggle were she to try to insert herself into the treatment before he was capable of having a truly spontaneous two-person experience. She understood that Arthur needed the resolution of his problems, if it were to come, to be experienced as *his* discoveries and resolutions, not hers. So she very carefully allowed Arthur his separate, one-person experience. The underlying transference–countertransference power struggle did need to ultimately emerge, but not for another 13 years. We hear it vividly illustrated in the session Kate just presented. Before then, however, Arthur needed to reexperience 13 years of preadolescent life in the enacted dimension of the treatment. More about this later.

Phase II: The Next Seven Years (Until Arthur Stops Treatment in December 2007)

As his more emotional and spontaneous self gradually begins to emerge over the next seven years, Arthur gets involved with G. Like Kate, G is able to maintain the distance and separation Arthur needs. The relationship lasts three years, and Arthur finally has successful intercourse. But he is still the observer in their sexual activity (and in the analysis), not a subjectively immersed participant. During this time he also starts to have business successes. However, both events leave him feeling depressed. Neither external event cures his damaged internal self-representation or the conflicts that torture him. He becomes increasingly angry and disgruntled, and Kate finds herself becoming more and more frustrated and combative, as well as contemptuous of him in her thoughts.

In August 2006, Arthur's father dies. Kate is away on vacation, and he experiences her as unavailable. Additionally, his major creative project — what was formerly an "impossible dream" — becomes a reality. He hadn't asked Kate to come see it, but he had wanted her to. Kate's absence for these two events become the treatment version — the actualization — of Arthur's earlier experiences of absent parental validation. He holds a grudge about the two events, using them to distance himself from Kate and, via projective identification, from his feelings of humiliation and self-contempt. He can no longer sustain the magical belief that an external success will cure him, and he can no longer maintain his strategy of not having feelings. The despair over his damaged self becomes more and more intolerable. By summer 2007 he starts to talk about stopping treatment, and he does so in December 2007. As I see it, this action is a complex enactment. (The two terms are not the same.) It is an *enactment* because it *actualizes* aspects of Arthur's internal world. Stopping treatment is the actualization of his developmental trauma, a defense against that trauma, and also an actualization of multiple transference motives, as follows: Disrupting his treatment after 13 years actualized the massive disruption Arthur experienced at age 13 (which was an adolescent edition of earlier developmental issues), when he was displaced into a new community with no help from his parents with the adjustment. It is also a defensive flight from the emerging passive-dependent/masculine-assertive conflict that that event ushered in. Finally, by leaving, Arthur was attempting to escape (as well as punish) the transference mother who could not allow Arthur's autonomous self-strivings, as well as the transference father who could not affirm his manhood.

Phase III: April 2008

So now we come to the momentous week last April, when Arthur returns to treatment. The attempt to propel himself into adult/masculine life on his own and avoid a slide into merger with his mother — again, an unconsciously arranged version of what had been thrust on him at age 13 when his family moved — has failed. And the defensive strategy he initiated back then — never to relinquish total control over his feelings — is also no longer working. Now in a serious depressive regression, he returns to Kate. In the first session, a Monday, he asks Kate to hold his hand. She does. On Thursday, he is in a comatose-like state on the couch. Kate holds his hand again and also sees him for two additional sessions that same day. After two more sessions, on Friday and Saturday, he begins to recover. In the following weeks, he tells Kate that he experiences her as a "big-hipped woman wanting intercourse" and also fears being sucked into a "big black hole." After a month of meeting on an as-needed basis, with Arthur now more or less recovered from the regression, they formalize once-weekly sessions.

Noteworthy during this week's sessions are the following: First, Arthur is able, perhaps for the first time, to allow himself to be totally dependent on Kate, asking her to hold his hand. This achievement was made possible, in part, by his having turned the *passively* experienced trauma of the family move at age 13 into an *actively* initiated move in the transference.

Second, as Kate was responsive to Arthur's earlier need to be sealed in his one-person cocoon, she is now responsive to his new need. Even though she realizes that during the first hand-holding (if not during the second one too) that Arthur is still an observer and not an experiencer, she is intuitively sensitive to the new transference–countertransference climate that these gestures are ushering in.

Third, the hand-holding moment, in which Arthur risked total "out-of-control" dependency and humiliating need, is also noteworthy for being the first spontaneous, two-person interaction that Arthur has ever had with Kate. As the months progress, Arthur is now able to feel and articulate his previously warded off terror of Kate as a sexual "big-hipped" woman who wants intercourse and a big black hole that will devour him. These are anxieties that had their roots in the early separation–individuation conflicts with his mother and later reactivated when he entered adolescence.

Fourth, as the month of April unfolds, Kate is freed from the one-person constraint that she too has long felt. She is able to articulate to Arthur her dilemma about how to raise the issue of regular sessions, and she and Arthur are able to negotiate a schedule, and a new fee arrangement, together.

And, fifth, most important, as they begin regular weekly sessions, in May 2008, Arthur and Kate are now able to enter the intense sado-masochistic relationship illustrated in Kate's process material. I see this not so much as a "transference–countertransference *muddle*" as Kate describes it – although I'm sure it felt that way. I see this session as illustrating the sado-masochistic features of the separation–individuation, anal-rapprochement phases of development that Arthur had not been able to successfully traverse either in childhood or in adolescence.

Phase IV: The December Session

Now to the December 2008 process material. It is now seven months into this new phase between Arthur and Kate, and the cat-and-mouse transference–countertransference struggle is in full swing. Equally important, we can also hear in this material Arthur's developing capacity to observe and struggle with his own feelings and conflicts, relating to Kate in a fuller way. I'll return to this in a moment.

On the countertransference side of the cat-and-mouse struggle, Kate is quite in touch with her own hostile thoughts and impulses. As Arthur repeatedly devalues and dismisses her, toying with her and baiting her, Kate feels enraged and frustrated. She is mostly able to contain her impulse to take the bait and "pounce," but she occasionally finds her irritation inadvertently emerging in the tone, or content, of her comments. The aliveness and intensity of this struggle between them is quite important for Arthur as it allows him to experience his aggression, Kate's aggression, and to see that they are both surviving. This will in turn open pathways for new feelings and further growth.

An important point I wish to make about the interactions in this session, and in the April sessions, is that Kate was not consciously playing a role, or consciously trying to provide Arthur with a particular kind of object-relational experience. Arthur's intense, regressed state of early dependency, and the ensuing separation–individuation/rapprochement struggle, both evolved naturally as part of the ongoing, unconsciously evolving enacted dimension of the treatment. When Arthur let himself place his psychic survival in Kate's hands – literally – and when Kate, in the context of this actualized state of early dependency, unequivocally met this totally new gesture of need, the conditions were ripe for Arthur to resume a process of individuation and growth. This was so because the object whom he had experienced, over many years in the transference, as a self-interested and ineffective mother, he had now come to discover to be different from this original early object in her ability to recognize his selfhood and meet his early needs as they emerged. Again, this entire treatment-long therapeutic process evolved unconsciously, in what I call the enacted dimension of the treatment.

Indeed, throughout the session Kate presented to us – even as Arthur is involved in the sado-masochistic cat-and-mouse game – we hear him simultaneously involved in a new object-relationship in which he feels able to observe himself out loud, and experience and share his feelings. A few examples:

- Arthur makes what is, in effect, an interpretation of the psychic dilemma he encountered when he prematurely left treatment. He reflects: "I survived, but then it's lonely." He is then able to reflect on his choices, now more conscious, of whether he should "keep digging" or "just cruise."

- Arthur is able to acknowledge Kate's existence and her importance to him, telling her that for the first time he is taking his vacation simultaneously with hers. He doesn't need to deny her importance by fleeing beforehand.
- Arthur now talks with more intensity about how let down and forgotten he had felt by Kate. And he has also achieved enough distance from these feelings that he can initiate a spontaneous, self-aware line about the meaning of his cat-and-mouse game – "You just can't win," he says laughingly. This creates enough space for Kate to respond, with mutuality, and in kind: "I'm aware of that – thanks for the interpretation."
- Arthur also struggles with having tender feelings for his nephew, his brother, and for Barbara, even as he expresses contempt for these same feelings. He is able to hear Kate's interpretation that he feels humiliated by these tender feelings, finds it hard to have them in her presence, and that that is perhaps the reason he needs to make sure that she doesn't feel she is of value – in other words, that he wants *her* to feel humiliated, not him.
- Most important, Arthur has experienced a change in himself: The next session begins with his expressing his pleasure over the "intensity" and "out-of-control" feeling he had had in that session, even as he tells Kate that he thought of calling her between sessions to tell her this – but decided not to.

"Enactment"

So let's look again at this concept of "enactment." What are the enactments in this treatment?

As I said at our last meeting here, "enactment" is not a particularly good term. It leads us to think more of discrete, behavioral events – like Arthur's stopping treatment, Kate's holding his hand, or Kate's inadvertent expressions of irritation and contempt – and it tends to have the negative connotation of stepping out of line. More useful, I feel, are process terms like "actualization" and the "enacted dimension of analytic process." These terms attempt to conceptualize what is actually a dynamically evolving, unconscious process. They focus our attention on how unconscious fantasies are playing themselves out in the analytic process in an inevitable and essential way.

So what was unconsciously actualized for Arthur in the enacted dimension of this treatment? As I touched on earlier, by stopping treatment after

13 years, Arthur recreated the trauma of his adolescent move to a new neighborhood when he was 13. By turning passive into active in this way, he could finally allow himself to relinquish the defensive strategy that he had instituted at that time, and to risk the deeper feelings and painful conflicts that this brought him. Returning to Kate, he was then able to experience the total dependency that he had been unable to experience with his mother, and could not previously experience in the treatment. When these early needs were met by Kate, he was then able to enter into the early developmental struggle with her to forge an autonomous, cohesive self through their relationship.

On the countertransference side, something about Kate as an analyst enabled her to allow Arthur many years of space to actively recreate his old experiences and find new solutions. Kate allowed Arthur years of isolation and self-regulating rituals in which to build his "sand castles," and the freedom to sit up or lie down at will and play with the frequency of sessions and vacation time in order to titrate the intensity of the transference. She was able to allow him to make that "peculiar arrangement" that brought the analysis almost unawares to an end, but, in its ambiguity and flexibility, also enabled Arthur to return.

In Lucia Tower's remarkably prescient 1956 paper on countertransference, she coins the term "countertransference structure" to refer to specific aspects of an analyst's character, or even a particular unconscious conflict, that becomes especially important, even crucial, to the actualization and working through of a particular patient's central conflict. Kate's capacity, throughout the treatment, to allow her patient to have his own experience and to make his own decisions, to unhesitatingly respond to Arthur's new gesture when he returned to treatment, and to be the feisty, combative analyst we see in the session just presented, fully engaging in the rapprochement struggle with Arthur, were especially important to this particular patient's need, and subsequent ability, to reexperience the isolation of his childhood, the breakdown in his adolescence, and the total dependency in the treatment that allowed him finally to begin the process of individuation and growth.

Finally, this unique *inter*psychic connectedness between Kate and Arthur is also evident in the "touching" that took place between them throughout the treatment. Kate's emotional in-tuneness was the continuous "light touch" Arthur needed, and Arthur's poignancy, particularly in the final hour before stopping in December, clearly "touched" Kate, as she said. These aspects of their transference–countertransference connection culminated in the *physical* touching in April, when Kate "lent him a hand," and developed into the spontaneous sparring and laughing touching we heard in the session presented that Kate had earlier likened to tickling a young child. This *inter*psychic connection, and Kate's ability to stay "in touch" with it, process it, and even occasionally lose herself in it, was a key feature, I believe, of her remarkable and impressive work with Arthur.

Note

1 The case of Arthur, and my discussion, were originally presented in March 2009 at the second of a three-part inter-orientation colloquium on enactment sponsored by the Contemporary Freudian track of the NYU Postdoctoral Program in Psychotherapy and Psychoanalysis.

10

THE ENACTED DIMENSION OF ANALYTIC SUPERVISION
The Parallel Process Phenomenon

Enacted processes are not only an inevitable part of analytic treatment, they are also an inevitable part of analytic supervision. In this chapter I will take up the enacted dimension of the supervisory process as manifested in what is commonly known as the parallel process phenomenon – the well-known observation that at times a supervisee may mirror, imitate, or reenact with the supervisor a particular behavior, dynamic, or conflict of the patient – and offer two illustrations from supervisory vignettes in the literature.[1]

The literature on the parallel process phenomenon has, in several ways, mirrored the general literature on action and enactment in analytic treatment. Early on "parallelisms," like "enactments," were treated as exceptional or transient events, viewed more as discrete epiphenomena during the supervisory process rather than as an ongoing part of the process. Additionally, from the time it was first described by Ekstein and Wallerstein (1958) over a half century ago, the phenomenon, like the early concept of acting out, was considered primarily from within a one-person or unidirectional framework. Most writers on the subject (Arlow, 1963; Baudry, 1993; Ekstein & Wallerstein, 1958; Sachs and Shapiro, 1976; Searles, 1955) emphasized a problem the candidate was having in the treatment relationship – the candidate's transitory identification with some aspect of the patient's conflict or defense – which then became paralleled (enacted), in a kind of carbon copy way, in the supervisory relationship. Others, like Doehrman (1976), emphasized how conflicts in the supervisory relationship became paralleled in the treatment relationship. Only Gediman and Wolkenfeld (1980), among the early writers, eschewed these unidirectional domino theories and proposed that parallelisms were the outgrowth of a complex *systemic* process, in which the point of origin was ambiguous or overdetermined.

As analytic theory expanded to encompass interactional and intersubjective perspectives, newer views of the parallel process phenomenon have also emerged. One of the first writers to embrace an interactive perspective was

91

Boesky (1995, unpublished). His view that parallelisms were co-created opened a window into the total situation, beyond the role of the candidate's conflicts alone, setting the stage for a reconsideration of the contributions of all of three participants. From a relational/intersubjective perspective, Berman (2000) considered three sets of dyads in the supervisory field: the analyst/patient, the supervisor/analyst, and the supervisor/patient. Utilizing Ogden's (1994a, 1994b, 1996) concept of the analytic third, Brown and Miller (2002) extended the intersubjective perspective further by considering how what they call the "triadic intersubjective matrix" may create a "supervisory fourth." All of these writers emphasized that the parallel process phenomenon – the *enacted dimension of analytic supervision* – is an integral part of the clinical data to be investigated during the supervisory process.

The following two supervisory vignettes illustrate the presence and function of the enacted dimension of supervision. While all three of the participants in each vignette contributed to the parallel process, I take the candidate as my focus and point of reference because the candidate, the intermediary between the supervisory and treatment settings, is the one who does the actual paralleling from one setting to the other. It is also the candidate who is the central focus of our educational effort, and to whom we must return to consider the educational use to which parallel process phenomena might be put.

Supervisory Vignette 1

This vignette, presented at the 1995 panel by Boesky, was written, and later published, by a candidate (Pegeron, 1996, pp. 699–701) who wrote of his own experience with the parallel process phenomenon, and as such provides an important perspective on the phenomenon.

Dr. A had been my supervisor for Mr. C for one and a half years. When Dr. A's wife became seriously ill, he decreased the frequency of our meetings to every other week. After her death, three months later, he took a month off. During that time I sent him a condolence card in which I told him that I had appreciated and admired his ability to be as available to me as he had been during this difficult time. I added: "My thoughts are with you." I felt this genuinely as I had not seen any significant change in his ability to supervise and as I imagined what it was like for him. I was also beginning to work on this paper which he had inspired.

On the day of his return he thanked me for the card though he had not yet read it. In a session I presented shortly thereafter Dr. A pointed out a number of ways in which I missed or deflected Mr. C's homosexual transference. This appeared in the context of the patient's loneliness on weekends. I found the supervision session helpful, and I began thinking about what may have contributed to my countertransference. My thoughts turned to the card I had sent Dr. A and to the slight discomfort I had felt about the fact that he had not commented on its content. I started putting together what my fantasies had been. I had been hesitant to express my thoughts on the card because I felt they revealed more openly my idealization of him. I had even wondered if I had been too "forward." Yet Dr. A had been particularly helpful to me in being more genuine with my patient, and I saw my openness with him as a direct expression of the fruits of our work. His not commenting on the content of the card revived my doubts. I now realized that I had imagined he was uncomfortable with my admiration of him and my expression of warmth because it was a bit "too close for comfort" and homosexually tinged. I saw the parallel in my patient's relationship with me and decided to bring it up with Dr. A, since in the past this kind of discussion had been very useful.

I began the next supervision session by giving him a check and asking him if he had sent me a bill. Since I had moved to a new office, my mail had not been delivered regularly. He said he had mailed it but recalled that even though I had given him the new address, he had sent it to my old address. I then shared with him the above thoughts. He commented at one point that he wondered why I had felt uneasy, because he felt I had acted as a good friend. I concluded my remarks by saying that I understood now that I had identified with my patient and attributed to Dr. A my own countertransference of which I had not been aware. He agreed with my assessment. He then added that in an indirect way I was also saying: "Dr. A, why don't you practice what you preach?" He said that by not being sensitive to the importance of my openness he was keeping me at a distance. He also reflected on our interaction at the beginning of the session and pointed out that his using my old address was further evidence of this parallel process and illustrated how the parallel process goes both ways.

As a result of this interaction I felt relieved, and I also realized that I had felt troubled and self-critical of my countertransference. To see it now, in action and openly discussed by Dr. A, enabled me to place it in perspective as part of the analytic work at hand and something that needed to be further analyzed. To borrow Oberman's (1990) words, this personal experience was related to the transference I had toward my supervisor. It was not just a neurotic residue. I could now use it as a tool of the trade and process it to understand better my countertransference and the patient's transference. It also gave me an opportunity to look deeper into the issues behind my being indirect with Dr. A. This led me to recognize that one of the aspects of my idealization of him was a reaction formation. It had been difficult for me to let myself be aware of feeling left out when he had reduced the frequency of our supervision because of the circumstances that made this change necessary. How could I be angry with him when he had to deal with his wife's imminent death? In part I was also identifying with the patient who felt lonely and left out on weekends. In the next few sessions with Mr. C, I found myself feeling more relaxed, more aware of homosexual themes and more comfortable interpreting them.

Supervisory Vignette 2

The second vignette is an account of a supervisory process published by Caligor (1981). It is a joint supervision of two candidates. Following is Boesky's summary of the process.

The patient, Helen, was a 35-year-old, never-married woman overly tied to her hysterical, sacrificing, and overprotective mother. Helen's father died when she was seven after a prolonged illness of several years. Helen was adopted at birth. She reported a recurrent nightmare. She is in her mother's house. She is involved with a man who is faceless. She gets close to him. He has power over her. She awakens terrified. In her life she avoids men or behaves with men in a masochistic, provocative manner, alternating between tearful compliance and demanding anger, always insisting she had been victimized. For two years she had been in a relationship with a married man, Mel, who was self-centered and inconsistently available.

In the first supervisory session reported, the candidate told the supervisor that he was upset because he was at an impasse with his patient centering on her relationship with Mel. Helen had had a lot of symptomatic relief in the treatment but there were two vexing issues. The first was her insistence on reducing the frequency of her sessions for financial reasons although she had simple and clearly available opportunities to increase her income to maintain the present frequency. The second issue was that Mel told the patient that he was less available to her. She was terribly upset. She knew he had only been available on a part-time basis but she felt victimized. At the beginning he was far more available. How could she trust him? But without him she would be lonely and depressed.

The candidate told the supervisor that he didn't know what else to do. The patient didn't want to leave Mel, she just wanted to complain. Why hadn't therapy helped her so that she *could* make a decision? No matter how hard the candidate tried to get her to look at her role in the interaction he got only swirls of words, floods of affect, and not much afterwards. The patient indeed did cut down the number of sessions. The candidate was exasperated. He wished Helen would go away. He didn't attempt very much to stop her from dropping he frequency.

At this point the supervisor tried repeatedly to get the candidate to focus on Helen's way of relating to Mel, but the candidate ignored the supervisor. He would seem to agree but it was merely a "yes, *but*" deflection. He interrupted the supervisor, changed the topic, and drowned out the supervisor in a swirl of words. The supervisor tried to focus on the similarities between the patient's way of relating to Mel and to her analyst, but the candidate could not hear it. It was only toward the end of the session that the supervisor felt that the candidate began to understand how he and Mel were in the same boat.

The candidate began the next supervisory session by apologizing for not confronting the patient more vigorously. The supervisor had asked him before to consider with her what she did to induce Mel to spend less time with her. The candidate felt that his failure to confront her was a failing of his caused by his need to be a nurturing, caretaking person. He had to protect people. At this point the supervisor reminded the candidate that the patient had told him she had a dream she could not remember. The candidate then related that the patient told him about the dream by saying, "Oh, I have terrible news." The candidate asked, "What's that?" The patient replied, "I had a dream, but I can't remember it." The candidate then said to the supervisor, "That's how we got into that thing about working. She said, 'I have terrible news. I had a dream, but I can't remember it.'" At this point the candidate said to the supervisor, "Oh, by the way, I didn't really think anything about what we discussed last time, about the problems." This was a reference to the ideas of the supervisor about what was going wrong with the case. He then added, "I just didn't feel like thinking about it." The candidate next reports that he replied, with irritation, to the patient's report of the forgotten dream by saying something like, "You're telling me in no uncertain terms you don't feel like working."

Following the candidate's report of his outburst to the patient, he indicated that he was aware that matters had gotten out of hand. The supervisor next continued rather aggressively to focus on the candidate's failure to recognize sooner how annoyed he had been with his patient until the second candidate in the room, the co-supervisee, interrupted the supervisor to complain that he was badgering the therapist in the same way the therapist had criticized the patient for not working. The candidate then said it was hard for him to really be directly angry with his patient. He didn't want to say to the patient that he was furious with her. He didn't want to get into that kind of emotional entanglement with a patient, acknowledging how strongly he felt. The supervisor then indicated his own problem in getting in touch with his irritation with the supervisee. The co-supervisee then intervened: "You people act as if it is within her conscious power that she should recall a dream [in order] to work better, [or] to talk about what's going on between the two of you. She can't really do that at the moment." Following this observation, the candidate had the courage to tell the supervisor that it went against his conscience to be angry with his patients and to confront them with the fact that they were making him angry. He then stated that he had trouble believing that because *he* had a feeling that this was necessarily induced by his patients. It might be his own problem. The supervisor agreed with this verbally, but then persisted: "The key issue . . . was . . . why didn't I say to you in that supervisory session, 'Hey . . . I'm feeling irritable'?" as that was when it dawned on him that this was also a key issue for the candidate as well as for the patient. It was shortly after this, that the supervisor said that for the patient to learn how she drives people away from her, the therapist would have to be "authentic" – he would have to share with her what he experienced her impact to be.

Discussion

I will focus on the enacted dimension of each supervision. While the two supervisors have distinctly different theoretical orientations and supervisory styles, the enacted dimension is a prominent feature of both supervisions. The two vignettes have the following features in common. (1) In each, similar conflictual issues, in *both* the treatment relationship and the supervisory relationship, had been active and ongoing for an extensive period, influencing the participants in each setting in a reverberating way. (2) In both vignettes, the candidate enacted a different aspect of his conflict in each of the two settings, supervision and treatment. Thus, the enacted dimension of the supervision served important expressive, defensive, and adaptive functions for the candidate.

Similar Conflictual Issues are Occurring in Both Treatment and Supervision

In the first vignette, the conflictual issue salient in both the supervisory setting and the treatment setting revolved around emotional closeness. In the supervisory relationship, the candidate had experienced, over a time span of several months, a gradual withdrawal on the part of his supervisor: Dr. A's wife became ill, and he had to decrease the frequency of supervisory meetings and, after his wife's death, to discontinue them entirely for a month. Upon the resumption of the supervision, Dr. A acknowledged receipt of the candidate's condolence card – in which the candidate expressed his professional admiration and a warm personal feeling of connection – but with the comment that he had not as yet read it. Shortly thereafter, the monthly supervisory bill that the candidate was accustomed to receive by mail – or, to put it differently, the "*male* contact" to which the candidate was accustomed – did not arrive, as Dr. A had inadvertently sent it to the wrong address. At about the same time these events were occurring in the supervisory relationship, similar issues were taking place in the treatment relationship. The transference issues that were developing in the treatment at this time included the patient's expressing his longings for the therapist when the treatment was interrupted over weekends, a development to which the candidate was not attending.

The overt manifestations of the underlying conflictual issue – the "parallelisms" – are as follows: First, the candidate "misses and deflects" the patient's homosexual transference as he had felt his expressions of admiration and fondness were missed and deflected by Dr. A, and second, the candidate expresses warm, personal feelings toward Dr. A during the time the supervision had been interrupted as the patient had expressed longing for him following weekend interruptions of the treatment.

In the second vignette, the issue that is common in both settings appears to be conflict over the expression of aggression: passive provocation versus provocative confrontation, compliance versus passive aggression. In the supervisory relationship, the candidate felt critical of his supervisor's theoretical belief in the inherent therapeutic value of "authentically" confronting a patient when that patient "induces" the therapist to feel anger. The supervisor's way of working was already quite familiar to the candidate prior to the supervisory meetings reported, as supervisor and candidate had been working together in supervision for some time. But the candidate denied his critical feelings, and passively complied with what he felt was his supervisor's too aggressive approach. Ongoing in the treatment relationship at this time, the patient's transference paradigm involved her masochistic provocative manner, her alternating between tearful compliance and demanding anger. The candidate felt conflicted and confused about the frustration he experienced with her.

The overt manifestations of the underlying conflictual issue in this vignette are as follows: First, the candidate deflects and thwarts the efforts of the supervisor through a "swirl of words" and affect in the same manner as the patient had expressed her resistance in the therapy hours; second, the candidate criticizes the patient for not working in treatment in the manner he wished as he had felt criticized by the supervisor for not working as he had advised; and third, the candidate frustrates and taunts the supervisor by telling him he did not think about anything they discussed in the last supervision as the patient had frustrated and taunted him by announcing that she had forgotten a dream.

If the two candidates could have verbalized to their supervisor what was going on instead of unconsciously enacting it, they might have said something along these lines: "I am having a problem with my patient. I can't articulate it because it is stirring up issues of my own which I don't want to acknowledge. But even if I could articulate it, I'd still have difficulty relating it to you in supervision because I perceive you as having a similar problem with these issues, and this has been complicating *our* relationship as well. Instead, I will express all of this in action. I am choosing this solution over others at my disposal because in this way I can express it and defend against it at the same time."

Different Aspects of the Conflict Are Enacted in Each Setting

In addition to the just mentioned expressive function, the enacted process in both vignettes took the form of a type of splitting in which different aspects of the conflict were enacted in each setting. In this fashion, the parallel process also served both a defensive and an adaptive function.

In the first vignette, the parallel process involves the separate and alternating enactment of seeking and withholding emotional closeness. In the supervisory relationship, the candidate, in identification with the patient, seeks closeness through his comments in the condolence card and in his eagerness to pay his supervisory bill despite the fact that he had not received it. In the treatment relationship, the candidate, in identification with the supervisor, withholds emotional closeness by missing and deflecting the patient's expressions of longing. By keeping the two sides of the conflict isolated and experienced separately in the two processes of treatment and supervision, the candidate keeps himself unaware of his conflictual feelings. Additionally, as Dr. A points out to his candidate, by enacting the conflict with the patient the candidate was both bringing it to Dr. A's attention – an adaptive function – and also indirectly chastising him for being distant with him – saying to Dr. A, as Dr. A put it for him: "Why don't you practice what you preach?"

In the second vignette, the defensive process in the candidate involves the separate and alternating enactment of passive and active forms of the expression of aggression. In the supervisory relationship, the candidate, in identification with the passively frustrating and provocative patient, frustrates and provokes the supervisor, initially by passively thwarting his efforts to help – the swirl of words – and then, in the second supervisory meeting, by provocatively dismissing him – not thinking anything about what they had discussed. In the treatment relationship, the candidate, in identification with the actively confronting supervisor, criticizes the patient for frustrating his efforts to help her. In this vignette too, the parallel process served expressive and adaptive functions: it allowed the candidate to express his frustration and anger toward both the supervisor and the patient, and it communicated to the supervisor, by rendering the supervisor helpless as well, the nature of his conflict and anxiety with the patient.

As I hope I have illustrated, the "parallel process" that occurred in each of the vignettes presented was not a single, discreet event that proceeded in one direction from the treatment relationship to the supervisory relationship. Rather, each was the outgrowth of *ongoing* issues occurring in *both* settings, a manifestation of the dynamically evolving, enacted dimension of the supervisory process. The enacted dimension is as inevitable, and as important, a part of the supervisory process as it is of the treatment process, and it is a potential source of data for investigation by the supervisory dyad. Moreover, the interpenetration of unconscious issues in the patient–analyst–supervisor triad allows the candidate's difficulties in the *treatment case* to become affectively alive in the *supervisory setting* in an immediate and powerful way, adding emotional conviction to the candidate's educational experience and analytic work. The candidate in the first vignette put it well: "To now see it in action and openly discussed by Dr. A enabled me to place it in perspective as part of the analytic work at hand."

Note

1 This chapter is an adaptation of my discussion of Dale Boesky's paper, "Parallel Process and Supervision." Both were presented at a Scientific Meeting of the Institute for Psychoanalytic Training and Research (IPTAR) (Beren, 2005, March).

Part III

TRAUMA AND THE ENACTED DIMENSION

The treatment of patients who have suffered severe trauma is of central interest to all clinicians. Work with combat veterans suffering from post-traumatic stress syndrome, and our increased sensitivity to the frequency of childhood physical and sexual abuse, have led to a burgeoning of clinical and theoretical interest in the subject. Further fueling this interest is the contemporary research in the field of cognitive neuroscience which has been able to delineate neurobiological processes, as well as areas of the brain, that correlate with the dissociative phenomena we see in patients who have suffered extreme kinds of psychic trauma and abuse. In analytic treatment, the enacted dimension is that realm in which such dissociated experiences – experiences that at the time of their occurrence could not be symbolized in words – find their expression and become potentially available for reintegration.

11

DISSOCIATIVE IDENTITY DISORDER AND THE ENACTED DIMENSION

As I indicated in Chapters 3 and 5, enacted processes figure prominently in the treatment of individuals in whose lives trauma and dissociative processes play a central role. It is important to keep in mind, however, that psychic trauma, as well as the dissociative mechanisms employed to cope with such experience, exist on a continuum. The kinds of trauma we encounter in our patients range from "small t" trauma, the kinds of environmental failures found in the Sandler and Renik vignettes described in Chapter 5 (the second being more severe than the first), to the kind of early physical trauma described in the Casement vignette in Chapter 6, to the trauma of object loss in adulthood (as in the case of Jimmy in Chapter 12), and from these to the more extreme kinds of "capital T" trauma such as that experienced by patients who suffered early, severe sexual and physical abuse, as will be exemplified here in the case of Sara, and the profound existential trauma experienced by survivors of the Holocaust (as in the case of Ann presented in Chapter 13).

Dissociative mechanisms employed to cope with trauma also range in their severity and in their impact on the individual's personality and functioning, from varying degrees of negation and denial, through the more extensive kinds of disavowal and splitting that lead to identity diffusion and poorly integrated self-states, to what we know as full-blown multiple-personality and dissociative identity disorder (DID), illustrated in this chapter. Even in the most severe cases of trauma, there are many forms of dissociative response. In their studies of Holocaust survivors, Dori Laub and Nanette Auerhahn (Auerhahn & Laub, 1998; Laub & Auerhahn, 1989, 1993) have delineated a continuum of eight forms of knowing/not-knowing about massive psychic trauma.

> The different forms of remembering trauma range from not knowing; fugue states (in which events are relived in an altered state of consciousness); retention of the experience as compartmentalised, undigested fragments of perceptions that break into

consciousness (with no conscious meaning or relation to oneself); transference phenomena (wherein the traumatic legacy is lived out as one's inevitable fate); its partial, hesitant expression as an overpowering narrative; the experience of compelling, identity-defining and pervasive life themes (both conscious and unconscious); its organisation as a witnessed narrative; to its use as a metaphor and vehicle for developmental conflict.

(Laub & Auerhahn, 1993, p. 289)

The enacted dimension of analytic treatment is the realm in which all forms of not knowing – the many ways that "small t" and "capital T" experience become dissociated and remain unformulated – enter the treatment and become available for therapeutic intervention.

This chapter presents the case of Sara, a woman with a DID and a history of severe childhood sexual abuse. The treatment process was presented as part of a panel discussion on dissociation (Frankel, 2007), at which the two presenters, Wilma Bucci and Siri Gullestad, as well as my discussion of their presentations, addressed the following questions: Is dissociation a built-in feature of our neurobiological circuitry, an automatic mechanism evolution has provided our species to protect us from the threat of annihilation? Or is it better conceptualized as a dynamically motivated defense that operates in the context of preexisting fantasy, conflict, and psychological dynamics?[1]

Bucci presented her multiple code theory of cognitive development and functioning (previously summarized at the end of Chapter 4). To review, there are two neurobiological systems that encode our environmental experiences. The first, the *sub-symbolic (or nonsymbolic) organization,* is mediated by the thalamic–amygdalar centers and encodes input from the environment in visceral, motoric, and sensory forms, and then automatically sends them on to the emotion executing sites and/or to the symbolic processing sites of the higher level *symbolic organization.* This second system, the symbolic organization, is situated in the cortical association areas and the hippocampus, and it is the system that creates language, meaning, and regulates emotion.

The sub-symbolic and symbolic systems are independent and imperfectly integrated pathways for processing and encoding our experiences. They are inherently "dissociated." They are connected only partially and to varying degrees by what Bucci calls the "referential process." As development proceeds, we build up what Bucci calls "emotion schemas," the templates we use to organize new experiences as they are differentially registered in the two neurobiological systems. Emotion schemas are essentially self–object–affect units, what analysts would call internalized object-relations (or what D. N. Stern [1985] calls "representations of interactions that have been generalized" [RIGs], or what Bowlby [1969] referred to as "working models"). Severe psychopathological conditions are understood as the organism's attempt to regulate itself by continuously maintaining dissociations either *between* the two neurobiological processing systems of the emotion schemas – what analysts would call splitting of thought and affect – and/or by maintaining dissociations *within* emotion schemas, what we would call the splitting of self-representations or the splitting of object-representations.

Multiple code theory views dissociation as a normal feature of our neuro-cognitive circuitry, an automatic mechanism evolution has provided our species to regulate affect overload, maintain homoeostatic equilibrium, and protect us from the threat of annihilation. While dissociation, in this model, is not an exclusive feature of severe pathological responses to trauma, multiple code theory does provide an additional framework within which to understand these complex conditions and to fashion treatment approaches.

The consideration of dissociation by the second panelist, Siri Gullestad, was rooted in a traditional psychoanalytic perspective. She questioned whether a neurobiologically based framework alone, without being embedded within a broader psychodynamic framework, could account for the dissociative disorders we see in trauma victims. She noted that today's continuing polarization of these two conceptualizations of dissociation date back to Janet and Freud. While both saw dissociation as a "splitting of consciousness" related to the exclusion of unpleasant memories and/or ideas from awareness, their explanation of why dissociation occurred differed. In Janet's (1889) formulation, the "narrowing of consciousness" and *desaggrégation* (translated as "dissociation") in the normal function of cognitive synthesizing was a consequence of a lack of psychological strength (*misère psychologique*) that resulted either from genetic weakness or from traumatic experiences, or the interaction between the two. Freud, on the other hand, conceptualized the phenomenon of dissociation as an active expulsion of painful material from psychic processing, i.e. as a dynamic *defense:* "The dissociations have originated owing to internal conflict, which has led to the 'repression' of the underlying conflict" (Freud, 1913, p. 208). To simplify, Janet's focus was on *deficit,* Freud's was on *conflict* (Nemiah, 1998).

Acknowledging that dissociation may originally be a response to overwhelming external traumatic events and environmental injuries, Gullestad focused on how a dissociative pattern may also, at the time of occurrence and later, become integrated into other constellations of conflict and defense. Through the case of Sara, she illustrated how the patient's traumatic experience came both from without (from her father's violent sexuality) and from within (from its subsequent organization within her own evolving sensual and erotic feelings and fantasies). Sara's multiple personalities thereby came to serve not only a self-protective function but also various wish fulfillments and defenses against them. Understanding dissociation as a motivated defense thus implies the existence of an active, strategic agent. Gullestad's approach to the treatment of Sara focused on addressing the potentially strategic "I" with affirmative interventions aimed at validating the patient's self-experience and strengthening the feeling of agency. Approaches that invite multiple selves into the dialogue, she asserted, ran the risk of reinforcing fragmentation.

I will now present Gullestad's case of Sara (2005, pp. 642–648) as presented at the 2007 panel, following which I will provide some further integration of these two perspectives on dissociation, and illustrate the role of the enacted dimension in the clinical process.

Sara

Being Multiple

Sara was in her mid-30s when she first contacted me. Living with three daughters, one with serious behavioural problems, she had recently resumed her university studies. For a long time she had suffered from depressive feelings, anxiety, and an almost chronic sleeplessness, in addition to permanent muscular pains. At times, she had an overwhelming urge to finish her life. Also, an extensive use of tranquillizers, of painkillers as well as of amphetamine was revealed. Sara's life situation was characterised by huge social, economic, somatic and emotional problems.

Both mother and father sexually abused Sara from when she was a small child. Later, father continued to abuse her. The nature of the sexual abuse varied greatly. Sometimes he was extremely violent and brutal – the first time he raped her she was five. Sometimes he was a charming, tender and loving man that Sara adored. Her relationship with father was one of intimate complicity, and Sara had a continuous sexual relationship with him during adolescence and into adult life. Most significantly, the childhood abuse was covered by a façade of utter normality. Living in a big house in one of the city's richest neighbourhoods, the main rule of family life was maintenance of the façade. Behind the masquerade life was terror.

Sara lived with extensive dissociated states of mind. Each alter represents distinct memories and aspects of the past, special talents and knowledge, particular likes and dislikes and different somatic reactions. To give a brief summary, "Elise," deriving her name from the Beethoven piece that her grandfather, who was a pianist, taught her to play, is exceptionally musically gifted. In Elise, depressive mood states are prominent. "Elisabeth," a fearless athletic sensation seeker, performs risk activities that Sara's fibromyalgic body does not tolerate, whereas "Axel," the masculine component in the system, takes over in every situation which requires physical strength. Nothing and nobody resists Axel! "Mari," a specialist in sewing, makes artistic pieces of clothes and loves housewife duties.

"Helen" comes forward as a main alter. Helen is the one who had a sexual relationship to father in adolescence and adulthood – she is father's chosen bride. Being an exhibitionist and a "whore," she is a great seductress, whom no man can resist. Her sexuality is limitless; her history is one of unmitigated promiscuity. With a special, almost evil, pleasure she seduces attractive married men, especially talented, interesting ones.

These are typical examples of dissociation:

> Someone has been shopping, and I discover that my credit card is empty. Those tiger pants – *I* never wear cloths like that – it must be Helen.

> I wake up in a bed I don't recognise, together with a man I don't know. *I* did not come to his house; *I* did not sleep with him – how did I come here? Who came here?

Sara also describes how she experiences the onset of dissociation:

> I was driving a car and there was a police control. I'm terribly scared of the police – so I disappeared. Axel took over.

As a rule, dissociation takes place by her leaving the scene if the situation is somehow experienced as unbearable.

From the first time I met her, I was struck by Sara's attitude of indifference. It was like nothing really affected her. Being exceptionally intelligent, her observations of other people, including helpers, were sharp and precise. She had a keen eye for absurd aspects of interpersonal situations and commented on them with irony and wry humour, often with a self-derogatory tinge. Her stance, however, was that of an outside observer – as if she did not take part in the scenes she described. Her communication often had an arrogant flavour – conveying contempt as well as self-contempt. Sara's psychological position seemed to be one of superiority as if she was not participating in the common life of ordinary mortals. She was "above," as if saying, "I don't care about your petty affairs." Sometimes she could talk about her troubles with an almost cheerful air – reminding me of the position Freud (1893–95) named *belle indifférence.* This stance contrasted sharply with the facts of her actual situation.

The Letter

Several years into the treatment, Sara began writing to me between sessions; this was email pioneer time. The idea of "writing her life" had from early age been a comforting one: Sara harboured a secret ambition of becoming a writer. Also, written communications represented a possibility for conveying thoughts and feelings that were too difficult to talk about directly. The innumerable letters to the analyst represents a special kind of clinical material in Sara's treatment. Truly, these letters disclose that Sara was exposed to a psychological hell. That her mother actively participated in the exploitation of her as well testifies to the utterly confusing world she had to deal with. I will give an example of her description of her mother and father's sexual abuse of her.

> I'm in mother's bed, and I'm very small. Father is also there, and all three of us are naked. But I had the pyjamas on when I came there. Mother wants me to suck her tits, and I will not do that, because I think they are disgusting. They want me to suck father as well, and I feel that they try to make me believe that there is no difference. I get sick, and feel that I have to throw up, but it isn't allowed to think it is disgusting, because it is a game, and I'm allowed to participate. I know it isn't true, and that anyhow it isn't my game, and I think they are disgusting, but mother is more disgusting than father. I'm bad because I am unwilling, and therefore I do it, so that they shan't think that I'm bad or discover that I think they are disgusting. When they have finished, I must stay in their bed, but I don't want to be there. I can't tell them that. I lie in the middle, and it is uncomfortable lying in between the mattresses. I would prefer lying down under father's quilt, but know that mother wants me to lie under hers, and therefore I rather lie in between the mattresses, freezing, waiting for them to fall asleep, so that I can go to bed in my own bed.

In my discussion, I shall focus on how the event described in the letter has been defensively elaborated, as demonstrated by analysis of the discourse style. *"I'm in mother's bed, and I'm very small"* is present-tense retelling, serving to involve the listener. The episode is nevertheless described in a structured, dry, affect-less language, organised around temporal order and reasoning, emphasising causality. Thus, the text blends a first-person-involving present tense, suggesting a "relived as if present in childhood" memory, and a presenting of the event from an adult perspective. It would seem as an adult presentation masquerading as a child perspective.

A striking feature of the narrative is Sara's representation of mother and father's mind states and her complex reasoning about her parents' thoughts. She emphasizes that although they try to deceive her by making her believe that there is no difference between sucking a breast and a penis, she sees through their deception. Normally, recognising that other people's actions are motivated by their intentions, wishes, etc., is an expression of reflective functioning. However, in Sara's narrative one is struck by a lack of a hypothetical element; she has an almost direct access to the mind of the other. What is the function of this emphasis on knowing the other's inner world? The underlying message seems to be that she is *strong*: her mind is strong, her feelings are strong. Not least, she can't be deceived! An almost omniscient perspective is portrayed: she is anticipating everybody's reactions and taking her precautions. The subject pictured is above everything. Considering the situation she is describing, it seems warranted to say that we are dealing with a defensive explanation. The adult narrator presents the story in a way that keeps feelings of vulnerability at bay. Sara is the one in control.

Despite the emphasis on her ingeniousness and strength, the text nevertheless portrays Sara as the victim she in fact was; she was obliged to do what she did in the sex games with the parents. There is, however, no openly expressed accusation, and the reasoning quality gives impression of reflectedness. Sara has every reason to accuse her parents; the point is, however, that she does not! She does not *own* her feelings of anger and reproach and therefore cannot express them openly and directly. Instead, the story is told so that we – the listeners – get angry. The text comes forward as *covertly* accusatory. We are left with the feeling: "How can people do such things to children?" We bear the anger. She has only told us about a factual event. The conveying of disturbing information is utterly dry. Neither does Sara convey her real feelings connected to the experience. Certainly, she tells us that she *"thought"* they were disgusting. However, the description of emotional reactions seems a reported fact, rather than a feeling. Thus, what is strikingly absent from the story is Sara's own affective experience.

Analyzing texts such as those presented by Sara gives access to significant and relevant aspects of the *current* structure and function of the mind of the author, i.e. to how the individual functions in the present (Fonagy & Target, 1997; Sandler & Sandler, 1997). Specifically, a written text may reveal how a person having to deal with confusing and overwhelming events of abuse tries to regulate threatening affects. Summing up, the narratives of Sara reflect a pattern of affect regulation characterized by *distancing*. The temporally ordered, reasoned style that characterizes her letters is a discourse typical of so-called avoidant attachment patterns, characterized by dismissing of affect (Crittenden, 1999–2001;

Main & Goldwyn, 1998). What Sara cannot tolerate is to feel that *she* is angry, *she* is in need of comfort, *she* experiences pleasure, etc.

The distancing is embedded in a *"strong self"* pattern. Memories are distorted to give an illusion of own power, thereby denying real vulnerability. As demonstrated by narrative analyses of adult attachment interviews, this is a typical pattern in persons having faced traumatic events (Crittenden, 1999–2001).

It seems warranted to assume that the very extremity of distancing and control portrayed by the letters indirectly points to the intense affects that have to be warded off: Underneath the reasoned style the reader senses the sheer pain and terror of the abused child, needing to find a way to survive.

Countertransference

While the *content* of Sara's narratives of living as a multiple was lively, even dramatic, her stories, especially about dissociation, nevertheless had a "flat" quality. Events often were reported as something that just happened. The structure of the telling was an adding of happenings, like a reporter. One session she talks about a dinner with friends. They had a good time, something was said, and then, she tells me, *"I suddenly became dizzy and disappeared."* At this point she stops and looks at me. I get the feeling that I am given a package of events that *I* have to take care of. *Her* narrative is finished; the riddles of the story are there for me to solve. *She* bears no obligation to examine what she has told me. There is a striking absence of *"why,"* no spontaneous inquiry into own motives and intentions.

Presenting the dissociating as something that "just happens," clearly expresses that *she* (Sara) is not in charge. The underlying message seems to be: "How are you going to handle this?" By way of countertransference, I hear an implicit challenge: "Whatever you try – you won't be able to help me!" This voice – a voice of an old dialogue – seems to carry a message of revenge: the dialogue partner shall feel that the wrongs done cannot be undone. The object shall not be let off too easily! I also hear other voices. Less dominant but still present is a voice of triumph, the voice of a person who is able to turn everybody around her finger. And behind all the other voices, barely audible, there is a voice of a helpless little girl who is ashamed of crying. Thus, paradoxically, while Sara's narrative is lacking a wanting and intending subject, still, as a listener I get the feeling of being confronted by an ingenious subject, subtly staging a plot. The countertransference feeling is of a highly sophisticated strategist.

Dissociation as Protection

Both the letters and the analyst's countertransference reactions point to a tremendous need for mastery. Dissociation, a key component of Sara's control strategies, sometimes occurred within therapy sessions, providing *in vivo* demonstration of her way of protecting herself. It should be noted that in Sara's case, dissociation did not take the form of dramatic transformation scenes that make the observer shudder, reported by several therapists treating DID patients (e.g., Sinason, 2002). As I see it, the lack of spectacular switching to other alters in the sessions might indicate that the process, at least in Sara's case, is more guarded than one usually thinks: Sara controls "whom" she wants to display and not. Dissociation in her case comes forward as a more subtle mechanism.

In an aetiological perspective, the extreme defence against feelings is probably linked to a generalized denial of affect that existed behind the façade in Sara's family. For one, one was not supposed to cry. Indeed, Sara's first memory of dissociation is connected to being left alone at a summer camp at the age of three: She remembers standing outside herself observing, with contempt, a little girl crying. Neither was one supposed to feel lust. A preferred saying of mother was: "Women in our family don't feel sexual pleasure." Lastly, all kinds of anger were forbidden: the important thing was to *behave.* Thus, prohibition of affects was generalized. In a session, telling the analyst that she had just received a message from her physician that she had to undergo a painful operation, Sara expresses that she is afraid. The analyst comments that this is the first time she openly conveys her feeling of fear, and acknowledges that, "This is something new." Later in the session:

SARA: I can't bear it. I just want to disappear.

ANALYST: Yes. I can understand that. The fear overwhelms you, and you want to go away. And being able to dissociate means that you have a mechanism at your disposal that has been very efficient in protecting you. So no surprise that it is tempting to use it, as you have experienced that leaving your body makes you invulnerable against physical pain.

SARA: It's so important for me that you understand that.

This sequence illustrates the value of *affirmative* interventions contributing to a feeling of relatedness that Sara never had experienced (Killingmo, 1995, 2006).

Discussion of the Case of Sara

Dissociation and the Enacted Dimension

Both of the perspectives on dissociation presented in this chapter have an important contribution to make to our understanding and treatment of severe dissociative disorders. While each looks at a different set of data, and each conceptualizes at a different level of abstraction, there are important areas of correspondence between the psychoanalytic and the neuroscience formulations. I think it would be unfortunate to polarize psychoanalysis and neuroscience, as we are too often prone to do with theoretical controversies within psychoanalysis itself. The dichotomy of conflict vs. deficit, for example – which in the present context of trauma is recast as Freud vs. Janet, or mind vs. brain, or repression vs. dissociation – and the dichotomy of insight via interpretation vs. new experience via the analytic relationship (to which I will return shortly) continue to obscure more than they clarify. To my mind (and brain), we need not discard any of Gullestad's well-formulated conceptualizations of the conflicts, fantasy elaborations, and defensive compromise formations involved in her patient's extreme dissociative solution to her childhood abuse in order to accept Bucci's formulation that, on the brain level, there are corollary disruptions in the complex integration – what Bucci calls the "referential process" – of symbolic and sub-symbolic neurobiological systems within emotion schemas.

Perhaps when considering the mind–body problem, we should question the assumption, rooted in Cartesian dualism, that either "the mind" or "the brain" is the primary system and acts on the other. In other words, perhaps it is not useful to think in terms of psychological conflict "causing" physical symptoms, and/or physical stress or trauma "causing" psychological conflicts. Perhaps it is more useful to think about mind and brain not as separate entities that act on each other, but rather as a single complex integrated system – the "mind–brain" system. After all, the psychoanalytic model of mind and Bucci's neurobiological model of brain do share some basic commonalities.

For one, each model conceptualizes both a lower level of symbolization and a higher level of symbolization – that is, a sensorimotor, visceral level of encoding experience into memory, and a verbal level of encoding experience into memory. In psychoanalysis, as I noted in Chapter 4, Loewald (1976) delineated the "primary memorial system," the nonrepresentational, enactive form of memory, and the "secondary memorial system," comprising verbally accessible representational memory. Dowling (1982) refers to the former – that is, those memories that get encoded on the sensorimotor level – as "motor recognitions"; Bromberg (2003) calls them

112

"affective memories"; and Busch (1981) calls them "memories in action." Many other contemporary writers, most notably Jacobs (1991), have written about the ubiquitous other-than-verbal levels of representation and communication in the psychoanalytic situation. Despite the historical emphasis of "the talking cure" on verbal symbolization, we have now come to appreciate the extent to which the experiences of one's life are remembered and expressed in treatment not only in the psychical sphere but also, inescapably, in the action sphere. I will return to this in a moment.

A second commonality is that both the psychoanalytic and the neurobiological frameworks conceptualize psychopathology, at least in part, as a disruption in integrative connections between systems. While the Janet, deficit-in-the-brain, model looks more to genetic or neurobiological weakness and to the "*dis*-integration" of links, and the Freud, mind-in-conflict, model looks more to active, motivated processes within the dynamic unconscious, I believe most would agree that, broadly speaking, psychopathology results from some combination of both genetic/neurobiological factors that predispose *and* environmental factors that overwhelm and/or are psychically conflictual, and that both factors are intertwined and become progressively intensified and elaborated, organized and reorganized, by layer upon layer of additional meaning and conflict-based compromise formations, as illustrated by Gullestad, all of which build and rebuild the neurological encoding of what Bucci describes as the emotion schemas of the referential process.

This brings me to the other psychoanalytic dichotomy that I mentioned earlier: the debate over how psychoanalysis cures. Is it through insight achieved via interpretation, or through new experiences that take place in the relationship with the analyst? In brain terminology, this dichotomy can perhaps be formulated as follows: does the process of psychoanalytic cure occur through changes directly to the higher level cortical functions, or does it require new kinds of experiential input that directly affect the sub-symbolic system?

Throughout this volume, I have tried to show how both factors come together through an appreciation of the role of "the enacted dimension of analytic process." As I have described, analytic process comprises two interwoven dimensions: the familiar verbally symbolized dimension (free-association, interpretation, etc.), and the enactively symbolized dimension in which unconscious, nonverbal communications are continuously taking place and may lead to unintended actualizations of transference (and countertransference) wishes and defenses. Again, these are not dichotomous dimensions or processes, but are inextricably interwoven at all times. Within the transference–countertransference matrix, symbolic or attenuated versions (what Bromberg [2000] calls "miniversions") of the patient's core conflicts and conflicted object-relations are inevitably created between patient and analyst. These spontaneous creations in analytic space are crucial ingredients of the therapeutic action of psychoanalysis because they are alive, shared experiences that link current and past experience with a vividness of affect that inspires great conviction. When they become conscious and worked through in the treatment, they create the kind of emotionally based, *experiential* insight that produces meaningful psychoanalytic change.

This conceptualization of analytic process and change would appear to have correlates in Bucci's neurobiological model of brain functioning. It would go something like this: in a good-enough treatment process, emotion schemas that have been encoded, early on in life, in the sub-symbolic system only or primarily, and continue to function automatically due to their dissociation from higher cortical processes, become reactivated with the analyst enactively – but within the structure and safety of the analytic frame. This allows analytic work to gradually build up new connections and associations in the cortical system (via the hippocampal pivot) creating new, more adaptive, emotion schemas.

To illustrate these ideas in the treatment of Sara, I would suggest that her extensive use of email communication (at that time an uncommon form of communication) was the external manifestation of an important transference–countertransference process taking place in the enacted dimension of the treatment. While Gullestad represented a potentially new, benign object-relationship for the patient, she was also still being experienced as an old, traumatic one. Communicating by email was Sara's enacted way of recreating and maintaining her lifelong dissociative solution to her trauma, while at the same time tentatively utilizing her analyst to finally begin the process of integration.

In the particular email cited in the case report, Sara describes not only being abused by both parents, but also her impossible position of having no adult figure to turn to, of having to "lie in between the mattresses, freezing, waiting for them to fall asleep, so that I can go to bed in my own bed." This email, as do her subsequent verbal reports within sessions, communicates only dry, intellectualized details of her memories, while the emotional experience of the trauma remains dissociated and unavailable. Sara's still "frozen" affect is, however, experienced in the countertransference, where it is symbolized and held in Gullestad's mind. She bears the affect for Sara until the session in which Sara reports feeling "afraid" about having to undergo a painful operation. "This is something new," comments Gullestad. Perhaps in unconscious recognition that Sara may also be referring here to the painful work she must yet undergo in the treatment – or to put it a little differently, that Sara is now beginning to experience painful dissociated affect *within* the sessions – Gullestad is able to link

Sara's lifelong dissociative defenses to the overwhelming affects that were their source, within the framework of an affirming and empathic intervention. Sara is able to accept this well-timed interpretation, a first step in the process of modifying internal self and object representations. Perhaps now Sara will be able to venture beyond her split, dissociated position "between the mattresses" – where she is a prisoner of her parents' neglect and abuse, their "complicitous victim" – and create her own "bed" in which she can begin to unfreeze, reconnect to her strangled affect, and then gradually, painfully, work through the many layers of conflict and defense that compromise her emotional functioning.

To once again put this in brain terminology: through the safe, gradual reactivation of the sub-symbolically encoded affects that have been dissociated from the events recorded in the symbolic system, affects and memories may now be able to become reconnected in the higher cortical association centers and then be offset, at least partially, by their gradual relocation within new emotion schemas built up through the analytic work.

My primary purpose in this chapter has been to illustrate the role of the enacted dimension of analytic process in the treatment of a patient suffering with a severe DID that had its roots in traumatic childhood sexual abuse. I have also highlighted some potential ways to integrate the contributions to our understanding of dissociation made by contemporary research in cognitive neuroscience and the more traditional dynamic formulations of psychoanalytic thinking.

In the next chapter, the case of Jimmy will illustrate how a traumatic object loss during adolescence – the sudden death of the patient's father, disavowed at the time of its occurrence – became recreated in the enacted dimension of the treatment, thereby enabling it to be emotionally processed for the first time.

Note

1 An earlier version of Siri Gullestad's paper was presented at the Joseph Sandler Conference on Dissociation, New Orleans, March 2004, and published in 2005 as "Who is 'who' in dissociation? A plea for psychodynamics in a time of trauma," *International Journal of Psychoanalysis*, 86, 639–56. An expanded version of Wilma Bucci's paper was published in 2007 as "Dissociation from the perspective of multiple code theory, Part I: Psychological roots and implications for psychoanalytic treatment," *Contemporary Psychoanalysis*, 43, 165–84.

12

OBJECT LOSS AND MOURNING IN THE ENACTED DIMENSION

The vignettes presented in Chapters 5 and 6 illustrated how early preverbal traumatic events may be recreated and relived in the enacted dimension of the treatment. In this chapter I will describe how a consciously acknowledged, but simultaneously denied, adult trauma – specifically a devastating object loss during adolescence – required an extensive period of time for the trauma to achieve symbolic actualization within the transference–countertransference matrix before the patient could emotionally acknowledge and mourn the loss.

For unpredictable periods of time – weeks, and on one occasion, three months – this patient did not attend his sessions. He never formally stopped his treatment nor did he ever indicate that he would not be coming. Rather, he would simply not show up. Attempts to analyze with him the meaning of his absent behavior had little effect, and at times only intensified it. The absent behavior had its roots in the death of his father, who died while away for six months on business when the patient was 15 years old. In the enacted dimension of the treatment, the patient recreated the absence and loss, over time, through an identification with his father as abandoner. An interpenetrating countertransference receptivity allowed the patient's actions to engender within the analyst the patient's disavowed experience of the trauma – the uncertainty and anxiety of waiting, the deprivation and despair of loss, and finally the immutability and finality of death. The analyst's eventual giving up on the patient's return – the culmination of this treatment-long, unconsciously negotiated transference–countertransference process – created an analytic version of the original traumatic death. As the enacted dimension of the treatment was gradually brought within the verbally symbolized realm, the patient began the initial stages of mourning for his father, now more in consciousness instead of action.

Jimmy[1]

Jimmy walked into my office two weeks before the anniversary of his father's death eight years earlier. I was to remain unaware of this connection for some time. Jimmy was 15 when his father died, and while he appeared in my office at the age of 23, in many ways he had not aged: he had a chubby, boyish face; his clothes were unkempt; and his manner was halting, shy, and insecure. He carried with him a large cup of soda from which he sipped regularly. While he did mention his father's death during that first consultation session, it was not his primary preoccupation. He came to therapy because he was unemployed and still living with his mother and sister, his girlfriend was breaking up with him, and he suffered from vaguely described symptoms of alienation, depersonalization, and dysphoria. His affect was flat, and he seemed lost and unfocused, a character unformed. He stated that he could come to treatment only once a week because he had little money. I recommended twice a week and offered to see him for a modest fee. He agreed to my recommendation but overslept and missed our next session, a prelude of what was to come.

Jimmy was a middle child, with an older and younger sister. His father was an architect and contractor who designed and built large housing developments. He was on-site on a long-term project in California when he died of a massive coronary. Jimmy revered his father but was also terrified of his volatile and sadistic temper. He was a stern disciplinarian and ran the household with what Jimmy described as "the strict rule of law." Jimmy longed for his father's pride and love but felt he received derision and criticism from him instead, making him feel inadequate and unworthy. Jimmy's mother was a needy and narcissistic woman who was overprotective and seductive in her attentiveness to her only son, an attitude that intensified after the father's death.

Over the course of the first nine months of treatment, a picture emerged of Jimmy as a young adolescent boy struggling to achieve a secure masculine identification with a father perceived as powerful and dangerous on the one hand, and loved, idealized, and desperately needed on the other. He described his father's temper and the many occasions when he felt criticized and ridiculed by him; and he also described his idolization of his father along with fears of being homosexual. These fears had begun when he developed a dependent relationship with a male mentor at college, although he had never had any conscious homosexual desires or actual experiences. He felt anxious and overwhelmed living with his mother and sister, describing both the seductive pull of his mother's nurturance and sexuality – they watched television together in the evenings on her bed – and his own conflicted and confused feelings. His girlfriend broke up with him shortly after he began treatment because of his dependency on her, and

118

he was unable to decide on a career or get interested in any job. He wanted to become a stand-up comic but could not take any steps to implement the desire. (I must add that he was in no way funny.) He began living an itinerant existence, alternately living at his mother's house and at the homes of friends and relatives until they asked him to move. He was passive and dysphoric, staying up late into the night, overeating, smoking cigarettes, drinking beer, and watching old movies on TV, and then sleeping late into the afternoon, allowing whole days at a time to pass him by.

The transference during this early phase was silent but intense. I gradually became aware that he felt quite afraid of me, attributing to me sadistic and sexual motivations. His own anger and homosexual wishes were rarely brought directly into the treatment. They were instead projected in this fashion, causing him to feel painfully constricted and blocked, often unable to articulate his thoughts. Most important, from the beginning of the treatment Jimmy often came late, missed sessions without calling, paid erratically, and bounced checks. His attitude toward this behavior was one of chagrin, self-blame, and helplessness. He could not understand why he kept doing it or how to change it. His responses to my attempts to interpret the motivation in his behavior were contradictory. At times, he seemed to understand that his actions were provocative, recreating the relationship with his critical and angry father. At other moments, even within the same hour, he seemed genuinely confused and disoriented, unable to comprehend what I was saying, unable to organize or articulate his thoughts. What did not vary, though, was the behavior. It persisted and intensified despite my attempts to keep it in the forefront of our work.

Toward the end of the first year Jimmy's debt to me had reached an unmanageable level. He was impulsively spending any money he earned on indulgences and acquisitions – junk food, alcohol, cigarettes, a second-hand car – and he was unable to attend sessions on any consistent basis. I felt that the treatment could no longer be sustained productively as long as his indebtedness continued. I discussed this with him and he appeared to understand and agree with my assessment. We agreed to suspend the treatment until he could repay what he owed.

He did not, however, respond to my bills for several months, and I felt I had to inform him that I might have to pursue legal recourse. This counteraction on my part quickly produced a phone call from him and a desperate plea for my patience. I received a check shortly thereafter. Unbeknownst to me it arrived on the anniversary of his father's death, which was also the anniversary of the start of our work together a year earlier. I received a check from him approximately every other week for three months until his bill was fully paid. I did not hear from him again until the summer, a month later, when he called to ask if he could resume

119

his treatment. We had five appointments scheduled prior to the August break. He missed the last two.

When we resumed in the fall, Jimmy decided on his own to use the couch and to regulate his finances by paying me after each session. I commented on his effort to be responsible and to safeguard our relationship and agreed to his suggestion, keeping my questions about this procedure on the back burner.

This second phase of the treatment lasted from that September until the following July. It was characterized by a general, but far from complete, diminution in the frequency of his missing sessions and a greater involvement in the treatment. Over the first several months he attended consistently and paid me regularly. Gradually, he began missing about a session every other week. Over the four months preceding the August break, he missed sessions more frequently, up to half of his appointments, but he paid me his entire debt when he did come.

The content of the sessions during this phase centered more consistently on his relationship with his father and with father-substitutes at work. During his seven-month absence from treatment, he had worked full-time in an established restaurant as a waiter and bartender. He expressed ambivalence about being a waiter, but he was liked by both the owner and the maître d' and was being groomed for a more responsible position. He spoke often of his desires and his confused feelings toward these two men – his need for their approval, his feelings of intimidation, his confusion and inability to assert himself – which led us to various facets of his relationship with his father while growing up.

However, he still found it almost impossible to talk about his feelings or reactions to me. He seemed to understand and benefit from my interventions, yet alternately and even simultaneously seemed to be completely perplexed and disoriented. In addition to his steady employment and the displaced transference arena it provided for our work, there were other improvements in his life. He stopped his drinking and he moved into his own apartment, ceasing his itinerant living arrangements.

Jimmy's depressive symptoms, however, continued unabated – feelings of despair, meaninglessness, suicidal thoughts and fears – along with fears of losing control of what he called "a powerful rage," which he did not understand and could not further articulate. I gradually began to pay more attention to the fact of his father's death and to his apparent incomplete mourning, and to the ways in which this intersected with the adolescent conflicts with his father prior to his death. But attempts to connect his feelings and symptoms to his father's death, while never rejected, did not go anywhere either. Moreover, as these issues began to emerge more in the treatment during the early spring of that year, he began to miss sessions again.

The increasing irregularity of our meetings made it difficult for me to maintain the continuity of the process, but Jimmy, in contrast, seemed to be able to easily pick up where he had left off two or three weeks earlier. I struggled with frustration, with doubts about the viability of the treatment relationship, and with continual technical quandaries about whether and when to call him when he disappeared for two or three sessions at a time, and how to bring this up without engendering an intensification of his absences. I became aware that he was making me wait for him as he had been forced to wait for his father when he was away in California, and was making me feel the frustration of not being able to do anything about it, as he too had no doubt felt. My interpretations along these lines had the same effect as before: he seemed to understand, but his behavior did not change. Indeed, his absences were about to increase exponentially. He did not show up for any of his appointments during the month prior to the August break.

A Dramatic Event

I called him toward the end of the month to let him know I would be away. He apologized for not attending his sessions, said that he wanted to come, asked for an extra appointment, then did not show up. After he missed his first session following my return in September I called him again, at which point he once more apologized and assured me he would come next time. He did not come then and I continued to wait, session after session, as three more weeks passed.

It was now late September, almost three months since I had last seen him. I had gradually become less preoccupied with the treatment and with what I should do, although I continued to hold his time. Then one evening as I was closing the office, I was startled to realize that I still had one more patient scheduled: Jimmy. As I reflected on my lapse, I realized that I had given up hope on the treatment. "It's about time," I admonished myself. "This has clearly never been any kind of viable treatment." I decided that I would wait out this last session and then write it off as a failed case. After 35 minutes I was about to leave when the doorbell rang. When I went out to the waiting room Jimmy greeted me with a slightly self-conscious but nonetheless warm and familiar "hello." It was as if he had returned from the grave, come back to life. He entered the office, took his place on the couch, and picked up where he had left off.

He was contrite and apologetic about not coming for so long, said he had some of the money he owed me and asked if it would be OK if he paid me the remainder in installments over the next few weeks. He then went on to consider, without being asked, why he had not come for three months. He stated, in his halting way, that it was perplexing to him because he had thought of coming all the time, planned on it every evening prior to a session, but never seemed to be able to make it. I was stunned to hear this as I had so irrevocably lost all sense that there was any connection at all remaining between us. He asked how long it had been. He reflected on the time period of three months and said, "Now that I'm thinking about it, three months was how long it was between the last time I saw my father and when he died." As I continued to listen in amazed silence, he went on to inform me, for the first time, that his father had been away for a total of six months. He had left for California in September, Jimmy visited him three months later over Christmas, and he died three months after that in March. There had been *two* three-month absences. Jimmy then reflected on the fact that it was now the end of September, the time of year his father had first left him. Aware now of the induced source of my counter-transference experience of having given him up for dead, I commented to him that he returned on this day to undo his father's departure, and that perhaps he had not come for three months to recreate his father's absence and that he returned to undo his father's death. I also commented on how he "thought of coming all the time." I told him that it was quite striking – and quite meaningful – that despite our not seeing each other for so long his experience of our relationship did not change, that despite the fact that he did not come or call he never doubted that I would be here waiting for him. He nodded his agreement and so ended our ten-minute reunion.

Jimmy did not come for his next session. In the following session, he stated, with much difficulty, that he was angry at me. He was angry, first, because I did not seem to sufficiently appreciate his efforts at setting up a payment schedule (he had wanted more approval and support from me); second, because I seemed not to have known that his father had been away for six months (it didn't seem possible that he had never told me); and third, because of my comment about his never doubting I would hold the time for him (he experienced this comment to mean that I might not have held the time and that I had doubted his commitment). I commented that he seemed to fear that, in one way or another, I would not be available to him, that I would fail him in some way or abandon his treatment. He agreed, comparing it to the time the treatment had been suspended: in his words, "the time you kicked me out for six months." He described how hard that period of time had been for him, how painful it felt to be "cut off" that way. I asked him about the "six months," since the time period had been closer to eight months, and he again associated to the six-month period when his father was away. I commented on how powerful and important his relationship with his father had been during that six-month period, how intact and vivid it was in his mind then and now, and how present it had always been with us in the treatment.

Aftermath

In the phase of the treatment following the time the enacted process became conscious, about a year, Jimmy still did not come regularly to his sessions, sometimes not showing up for weeks at a time, sometimes showing up 20 or 30 minutes late for the session. During the periods of waiting, I continued to struggle with the countertransference fantasies of abandonment and loss, although my greater understanding of Jimmy's need for this enactment, and my own reactions to it, made it easier to sustain faith in the presence of an ongoing and meaningful treatment relationship. In the sessions Jimmy did attend, memories of his father's death and its psychological sequelae emerged, and his life outside the sessions steadily improved.

On sporadic and discontinuous occasions, Jimmy described his sense of abandonment when he missed sessions. He imagined that, like his father, I, too, must feel critical of him for owing me money and that I should kick him out of treatment, "cut him off," as his father had done by taking leave of him. At the same time, he felt his father still owed him and that he should not have to pay for a father now. Other poignant enactments became verbally accessible: he mentioned that on his way to work now he often drove out of his way to pass through the housing developments that his father had built. He would park his car and sit looking for people he had known through his father. I commented on his efforts to keep his father alive and with him. In a later session, he told me of a time he had come late for our appointment and sat in his parked car across the street from my office for the duration of the session, looking at the light shining in my window. I likened this to his vigils in the housing developments, and asked him if he ever visited his father's grave. He said he had not been there since the funeral.

Midway through this year, after an absence of nearly a month, he called to say he wanted to "get back into the swing of things," pay me what he owed me, and that he would attend his next session. Two days later, my own father died. I called him and told him that there had been a death in my family and that I would not be in the office for the week. With emotion in his voice he said, "I'm very sorry to hear the news. I hope you're all right – as well as anybody could be under the circumstances." I was struck by the immediate connection he made with me, in such contrast to his usual halting, frightened, and blocked manner. I called after the week to confirm our next appointment, but Jimmy did not come for another two weeks.

When he did return, he stated that he felt like a liar for being in therapy but not coming. I suggested that perhaps he felt that I was the liar. I was his therapist but I was unavailable to him for a week. He repeated his concern about the death in my family. He imagined it had been my father and feared I would not be able to deal with my patients and would cut him off as a result. He worried whether his expression of consolation had been appropriate; he wanted to convey how much he felt for my loss. I told him that what he had conveyed had been heartfelt and that he seemed to understand something about loss very deeply. After a pause, he went on to say that he had been doing better – he had given up smoking, lost weight and was becoming more confident at work – and that he had been able to think about his father with more love and with less anger. At the session's conclusion, he paid me and said, again with more feeling than usual, "Thanks for being patient and for letting me be a patient."

Over the next several months, Jimmy was able to carve out a position as wine steward at the restaurant and to free up time for a social life. He also felt more assertive in his interactions with his mother. His grandfather died, his father's father, arousing his ambivalent feelings toward both paternal figures. He received a financial inheritance which he felt was a direct line from his grandfather through his father to him, but receiving money rather than love and support also made him angry. He related this to his unexpressed anger about wanting more from me and yet was also able to express gratitude that I had not given up on him.

Discussion

I will now describe the elaborately developed enacted dimension of this treatment process. I will describe how Jimmy's traumatic object loss was enactively recreated and symbolized in the treatment and the process by which this dissociated trauma gradually came to be integrated within the verbally symbolized dimension of the treatment. I will show how an unconscious, enacted countertransference process inadvertently intertwined with the patient's enacted transference to form this therapeutically necessary analytic version of the trauma, an experience that made possible the emotionally based, experiential insight (see also Bromberg, 2003; Chused, 1991, 1996; Jacobs, 1991, 1993, 1997) necessary for a resumption of psychological growth. I will conclude with some comments about enacted processes and analytic technique.

The Inability to Mourn and the Enacted Dimension

The process of mourning is a most difficult one, a process that even under the most favorable conditions is perhaps never fully completed (Freud, 1917). When the task of mourning must be accomplished by an immature ego, one that is still dependent on the object, the task may be nearly insurmountable and may take a long, circuitous route (see A. Freud,

1958; Jacobson, 1961, 1964; Lampl-De Groot, 1960; Wolfenstein, 1966, 1969).

Jimmy's father died at a crucial time in his adolescent development, at a time in his life when positive and negative oedipal issues were active, a time when his developmental need to have a father was vital (Blos, 1979). As an adolescent who had not yet consolidated his identification with his father, he lacked sufficient superego structuralization to do without the external presence of his father (Deutsch, 1937; Laufer, 1966). As a result, he was unable to accept the death and mourn his father's loss, remaining in many respects a 15-year-old boy, arrested in his psychological development in the midst of an unresolved negative oedipal struggle (see Altschul, 1968; Fleming & Altschul, 1963). Many of Jimmy's presenting symptoms reflected this arrest: his frozen affect, his stunted level of object relations, and his infantile ego ideal that resulted in pervasive vocational indecision, lack of initiative, and aimless dysphoria.

Jimmy's pathological solution to his dilemma was to disavow the experience of his father's death and to maintain its dissociation as he proceeded to live his life. Freud (1927, 1940a, 1940b), in his discussions of the dissociative processes found in fetishism, described the process wherein the individual maintained two contradictory beliefs simultaneously. Jimmy believed both that his father was alive and that his father was dead at the same time (see Altschul, 1968; Blum, 1983; Fleming & Altschul, 1963). From a cognitive-neuroscience perspective (see the discussion of multiple code theory in Chapter 11), this kind of dissociation can be understood as a disruption in the referential process between neurobiological systems, a disruption in Jimmy's capacity to integrate the intellectual knowledge of his father's death, encoded in the symbolic cortical areas of the brain, with the affective experience of this trauma that had been registered in, but had overwhelmed, the affective core of the subsymbolic neurobiological system. In the treatment, these dissociated self/brain states were evident in the erratic nature of his functioning within any given session: the way he could talk poignantly and thoughtfully about his father at one moment, and then seem detached and perplexed an instant later; and also the way he reacted to his behavioral enactments as if they were being done by someone else. Attempts on my part to connect his distress and his behavior with his unmourned loss were accepted in that self-state (or sector of his brain) that contained intellectual knowledge of his father's death, but did not register in the other, emotionally traumatized, self-state (or sector of his brain).

Whichever model one uses to conceptualize the dissociative process, when there is an inability to mourn a death – an inability to integrate emotional knowledge into the intellectual knowledge of the event – aspects of the traumatic experience will find expression in more primitive forms of enacted behavior and enactive language (Busch, 1989, 1995; Loewald,

1975), and will continue to organize psychic life side by side with higher forms of symbolic functioning. Bereaved individuals will tend to support the dissociated, emotionally inaccessible, reality by living out circumscribed segments of their lives as if the love object were not dead. When they come for treatment, they recreate aspects of their unmourned trauma in the enacted dimension of the treatment, regardless of whether or not they talk directly about the death.

In Jimmy's case, the enacted dimension of the treatment maintained the dissociation and denial of his father's death by reestablishing what was a six-month relationship-in-fantasy that preceded his father's death. His behavioral "enactments" – missing sessions and then showing up again, disappearing and reappearing – sustained and actualized an ongoing unconscious fantasy that his father was absent but still alive, transforming the treatment process and its participants into a living memorial of his unmourned trauma. Specifically, I will elucidate the underlying meaning of Jimmy's behavior in terms of the following: (1) denying time; (2) alterations in identity; (3) reversing the trauma; and (4) undoing the trauma.

DENYING TIME

When Jimmy's father died, the movement of time became dangerous. To be aware of time meant to acknowledge the end of waiting for his father, to acknowledge his death. Holding time still, on the other hand, meant he could remain waiting for a father who might return. So Jimmy stopped the clock and put his psychological growth, and indeed his whole life, on hold. He tried to reverse time – sleeping during the day and staying up through the night – in an effort to reverse the trauma. He was unable to adapt to the conventional demands of time such as maintaining a schedule or keeping appointments. No appointments kept, no date with death. He stayed up all night watching old movies on TV, involved in "reruns" of earlier times in his life.

Thus, in the treatment, each absence represented a retreat in time to the relationship he had had with his father in fantasy during the six-month absence – a "waiting-relationship" with an absent but, most important, a still living object. As it had been with this relationship-in-fantasy with his father, his relationship with me was most intense and most safe when he was *not* in sessions, when it remained a fantasy in his mind. Thus, after having been away for a long period, he was able to easily pick up where he left off because in *his* psychic reality, time had stood still and we had never really been apart. In *his* mind, we were alive and well and together. It was only I, keeping one eye on the external structure of the treatment, who experienced absence and the reality of time passing when we did not meet.

126

Put another way, Jimmy stayed away from his sessions because he could not yet tolerate his transference to me as the father of his adolescence who would die. The danger of abandonment and death was too real and imminent. Every impending weekend, every holiday, every vacation was a death waiting to happen. By absenting himself from treatment he could avoid a relationship with me which would, by definition, move forward in time, and therefore ultimately, in his mind, eventuate in death.

ALTERATIONS IN IDENTITY

Many facets of Jimmy's identity became concrete embodiments of preserving the pre-death "waiting relationship" with his father. Having been forced to "wait" for his father, in anger and unrequited longing, Jimmy became a "waiter" by profession. He "waited" in the restaurant, in boredom, impatience, and anger on the chance that his father would reappear, establishing relationships with the "regulars," the ones who did come back. Unable to experience the loss of his father, Jimmy not only became one of those individuals who continually misplace or lose their belongings (A. Freud, 1967), unconsciously repeating the loss, he became, from that moment on, the personification of loss: he became a "loser," a young man unable to accomplish anything with his life, stuck in a "loser" job, waiting on tables. And he became a "lost soul," lonely, alone, and unable to feel emotionally whole.

REVERSING THE TRAUMA

Jimmy sustained his fantasy of a relationship with an absent but living father by reversing the passively experienced trauma and identifying in action with his father, becoming reunited with him in the act of abandoning and depriving. As his father had abandoned him, so he abandoned me; as his father had deprived him of a needed relationship and an object for identification, so he deprived me by not allowing me to work and by not paying his bills. This "identification with the doer" (Segel, 1969), enabled him to recreate the trauma but avoid the suffering of being abandoned and deprived himself. His actions engendered in me his own disavowed experience of the waiting that eventuated in death. He turned me into the "waiter" and the "loser," and I experienced the same questions, doubts, and feelings about Jimmy and our work together as he had no doubt experienced toward his father and their relationship: *Did I have a patient? Was this a treatment? Was he coming back? Was the treatment over? Had it died?* On an unconscious level, in the treatment's enacted dimension, he was testing the safety of the process and my capacity to endure his trauma: "Can you tolerate absence? Can you tolerate interminable waiting? Can you tolerate death?" he was challenging. "If you can, perhaps I will be able to risk the pain of it also."

In the enacted dimension, Jimmy was also actualizing his fantasy of a reunion with his lost father. Throughout the treatment, in addition to missing sessions, Jimmy was repeatedly *returning* to sessions, his attempt to cheat death of its victory. Identifying with the aggressor and absenting himself from his sessions was an act of revenge and hostility; returning and reappearing was an act of reparation, restoration, and renewal. It was as if we were playing hide-and-seek, or an elaborate game of peek-a-boo (Frankiel, 1993). "Look," his absences were saying to me, "I am away and gone like my father, you can't get anything from me now"; but then, unexpectedly reappearing, he would add, "Peek-a-boo! Here I am."

From Enacted Symbolization to Verbal Symbolization

I will now focus on that day I so irrevocably gave up on Jimmy's return and he in turn reappeared. Although the trauma and accompanying transference fantasies (as well as countertransference fantasies, as I will presently describe) were being actualized from the treatment's inception, it was on that day that they finally became conscious in a way that allowed them to be symbolized on the verbal level. That day's dramatic events signified that an important shift *had already taken place* in Jimmy's intrapsychic balance – from the denial of his father's death toward its acceptance, from enacted symbolization toward verbal symbolization. As I pointed out in Chapter 3, dramatic behavioral "enactments," as distinct from the underlying unconscious fantasies being actualized, are often "lagging indicators" of psychic change that has forged ahead of both the patient's and the analyst's awareness. They are a wake-up call that summons the analyst to recognize that the enacted and verbally symbolized dimensions of the treatment are ready for integration.

All through the early phase of this treatment, although it was not recognizable at the time, Jimmy's abandoning and depriving behavior had actually been proceeding beyond the actualization of his fantasy that his father was absent but alive, toward the actualization of the very trauma he was trying to deny – his father's death. Through increasingly longer periods of absence, he was coming ever closer to letting the treatment die.

Over the same period of time, I was involved in an anticipatory mourning process for my own ambivalently held father who was in the advanced stages of Alzheimer's disease. In a sense, my father too was both dead and alive: present in body but absent in mind. This idiosyncratic parallel led to a countertransference disposition to the patient's unconscious fantasy, and an availability to be enlisted in his playing out of this fantasy. That is, I may well have been, in my unconscious identification with him, inclined to wait for Jimmy when he was absent in order to deny the impending loss of my own father. Or, from another viewpoint, I may have been reluctant to let go of Jimmy and become the depriving and abandoning father. Without being fully aware of it, the interpenetration of this counter-transference disposition (connected as well to issues at deeper levels) with Jimmy's transference press – what Sandler (1976) termed the analyst's role-responsive countertransference, what Tower (1956) called a counter-transference structure, and what Boesky (1990) called an unconsciously negotiated resistance – had made me increasingly able to tolerate the idea, far longer than I typically would have, that absence and waiting could be part of a viable relationship.

Within the enacted dimension of the treatment created by this shared unconscious fantasy of denying death, Jimmy extended his absence toward the symbolic three-month time period, just beyond the period of time he must have unconsciously gauged would be the limit of my patience, thus moving the treatment toward the recreation of a death, his father's death, represented in the countertransference by the day I so conclusively gave up on his return.[2]

Jimmy then returned on that day, to fulfill his unconscious fantasy of reversing death: both the death of his father and its enacted recreation in the treatment. But his return also signified a readiness to allow the dis-avowed trauma a measure of conscious, verbal representation. In Loewald's (1971) terms, the enactment had moved toward a "re-creative repetition" of the trauma in the sphere of the ego's organizing activity, as opposed to a compulsive reproduction of it. The analytic version of the trauma played out in the enacted dimension of the treatment constituted, in Freedman's (1994) terms, a "nonverbal transformation" of Jimmy's experience that served as a precursor to the alteration of his internal representational space. Further, the "shared fantasy space" created between us (see also Bach, 1994; Winnicott, 1971) now made transformational dialogue possible, leading to higher levels of symbolization.

These developments were evident at the outset of that session, when Jimmy spontaneously brought up the symbolic meaning of his three-month absence, as well as new information about the six-month absence that preceded his father's death. I had temporarily experienced the loss he was trying to disavow in my reaction of giving up on the treatment. But when Jimmy unexpectedly returned, my recognition of the event's meaning, in interaction with Jimmy's readiness to understand and accept it, allowed my verbal representation of the enactment – the interpretation of his unconscious fantasy of undoing his father's death – to finally have mutative effect.

My comment to Jimmy during this sequence – that there was something to be understood about his never doubting that I would still be there – implied that important relationships *can* end, and that it may not make sense to assume that an abandoned relationship can always or so easily be resurrected. I implied in it that I had doubted – that I had not shared his denial of reality and unreciprocated commitment to a relationship – I had doubted, and by implication had despaired and suffered when he had not returned for so long. Not surprisingly, confronting his denial of death had made him angry, but he tolerated this affect without having to disavow it. Specifically, for the first time Jimmy was able to talk about his anger with me over the earlier "six-month" hiatus in the treatment, and he was able to relate this experience to his father's six-month absence and death.

This shift from enactive symbolization to verbal symbolization marked the beginning of a process of integrating and working through experience that had previously been disavowed. This process was, initially, a *formative* psychic activity, one in which new internal representations and object relationships were constructed as dissociated states were gradually integrated, rather than one characterized by an undoing of a repression followed by the recall of a once-conscious representational memory. It had been made possible by the unwitting creation of an analytic version of the patient's trauma in the enacted dimension of the treatment, a treatment experience that was crucial to making it accessible to verbal symbolization and meaningful insight. Jimmy's ensuing process of fully accepting the trauma, which involved the working through of the many layers of conflict, defense, and psychic meaning that had subsequently been attached to the death of his father, was predictably slow and uneven. Despite a growing capacity to experience and contemplate his father's death, there were times when the dissociated state in which his father was still alive continued to find expression in action and behavior. During this phase of treatment I continued, now consciously, to contain the awareness of the disavowed trauma on his behalf and bear his absences without rushing to comment or interpret.

As this phase proceeded, time began to move again in Jimmy's life. He brought in a large appointment book one day: his attempt to acknowledge the reality of time and to invest in the reality of living in the present. He began to look physically older and more mature, as if the aging process had resumed. Relationships with people began to deepen, and he started a serious relationship with a new girlfriend. When he thanked me for "letting him be a patient," he was acknowledging that he *was* a patient, as opposed to an abandoned boy or an abandoning father. He began allowing himself more memories of his father and, in his dreams, the psychic representation of his father's age was no longer fixed at the age he had been when he died. During sessions, he began to feel pressure and itching in his eyes – the physical sensations of grief. And he visited his father's grave for the first time since his death, the symbolic action of acknowledging death.

Concluding Comments

I have illustrated the enacted dimension of analytic process as it occurred in this dramatic case of a patient traumatized by the loss of his father in early adolescence. The patient's necessary task of completing the mourning process required a preliminary period during which he literally recreated absence and waiting within the transference–countertransference relationship. In short, he replaced one external reality (death) with a less traumatic external reality (absence) and then created concrete experiences of absence and waiting to support his fantasy that his father was alive. His effort was to enlist me as a witness to this new reality (see Boesky, 1982; Reis, 2009) and for it to remain an unalterable "fact," unamenable to interpretation, for a symbolically meaningful period of time. An ongoing countertransference receptivity to the enactment ultimately allowed the death itself to find symbolic actualization in the treatment, following which it could begin to be symbolized verbally and integrated into conscious experience.

With patients who are less traumatized and more able to symbolize verbally, such dramatic behavioral enactments do not typically form the ongoing foreground of the treatment. Nevertheless, unwitting actualizations of transference (and countertransference) wishes and defenses are continuously woven into the fabric of the analytic process, emerging into awareness in the form of seemingly discrete "enactments" as developing psychic transformations in the treatment allow or demand. Such processes within the enacted dimension of the treatment fashion an attenuated, symbolic version – a living analytic version – of the patient's central conflicts. As lived-in experience, these "original creations" (Poland, 1992) between patient and analyst infuse the patient's core conflicts with the immediacy and affective vitality necessary for effective interpretation and ultimate integration within the verbal sphere.

As I discussed in detail in Chapter 8, our increased awareness of the ubiquity and importance of the enacted dimension of analytic process does not, in and of itself, necessitate or justify calls for the abandonment of the basic treatment model or the technical guidelines that constitute the analytic frame. To reiterate, enactments are not a component of technique; they are the observable aspect of an unconscious process – an unconscious transference–countertransference process – that is continuously evolving. Enactments are *unintended, but dynamically meaningful, departures* from the optimal analytic attitude that technical discipline, however defined, is intended to promote. They will occur regularly in every treatment, regardless of the analyst's conscious technical stance, whether it be strict adherence to standard technical principles, or abandonment of these principles in favor of a more spontaneous and deliberately interactive style. Any technical approach can be psychically appropriated and organized by enacted transference–countertransference processes.

To illustrate, both technical approaches I took with Jimmy – setting a limit on his disruptive behavior by suspending the treatment (as in the early part of the process), and then allowing these behaviors to continue (as in the process leading up to the dramatic session) – had an additional level of meaning, for each of us, in the enacted dimension of the treatment. Jimmy experienced my suspending the treatment as an actualization of his father's leaving him for "six months" and then, later on, he utilized my tolerating the absences to enact a reversal of this trauma (leaving *me* for the symbolically significant period of time) until he could recreate the death itself and then undo it (by returning that fateful day). On my end, neither technical approach was a simple matter of conscious or rational technique. Each was shaped, in significant degree, by enacted processes. Each was an unconscious compromise formation, fashioned out of Jimmy's pressure toward transference actualization and the press toward actualization of my own interpenetrating countertransference. Each technical decision, as well its timing, was part of an unconscious transference–countertransference drama that was unique to our particular unconscious, interpsychic fit. They were part of the enacted dimension of the treatment.

Notes

1   This treatment case was first presented at the 1993 Division of Psychoanalysis (39) spring meeting, under the title, "A Death in the Countertransference: A Patient's Unconscious Enactment of Object Loss in the Analytic Relationship" (Katz, 1993). An earlier version of this chapter was published previously as "Missing in Action: The Enacted Dimension of Analytic Process in a Patient with Traumatic Object Loss," in R. Lasky (Ed.), *Symbolization and Desymbolization: Essays in Honor of Norbert Freedman* (pp. 407–30), New York: Other Press, 2002, Chapter 18. The treatment segment reported is the initial two-year period of a psychoanalytic psychotherapy that enabled the patient to later enter a traditional psychoanalysis. It is not intended as a full case history.
2   To again distinguish the unconscious interpsychic aspects of this process from its overt, behavioral manifestation and from what is commonly referred to as "co-creation" (see Chapter 7): Jimmy and I each had our own version of the fantasy, each with its own genetic roots, unconscious dynamics, and subjective experience; what was uniquely "co-created" by our particular analytic dyad was the overt form taken by their interpenetration – the atypical and extreme forms of absence and waiting.

13

TRANSGENERATIONAL TRANSMISSION OF THE HOLOCAUST TRAUMA IN THE ENACTED DIMENSION

Much has been written about the psychological effects of the Holocaust on those who directly experienced and survived it, as well its effects on subsequent generations. Through the case of Ann, a third-generation survivor, Michal Talby-Abarbanel illustrates the evolution of an enacted process in which her patient's unconscious relationship with her mother's disavowed Holocaust trauma was recreated in the treatment. My discussion is based on her written report well as my supervisory experience of the treatment.[1]

Ann

Secretly Attached, Secretly Separate

Ann is a 32-year-old Jewish woman, a painter. She was raised in France and immigrated to the USA several years ago. In our first consultation session she told me that she had considered entering treatment for several years, as she was aware that since she left home, ten years ago, she has been experiencing complicated emotional processes she needed to work through. She felt she needed someone to help her to reach better integration. She told me in the first session: "My experience is sometimes like I have many parts to myself that I need to put together."

I could feel Ann's unintegrated parts through her appearance and the way she dressed. Her somewhat sweet and childish voice did not fit her mature and strong presence. She dressed in a Bohemian style, an amalgamation of contemporary fashion with old-fashioned items that looked as if they belonged to a different period. I learned later that these antique dresses belonged to her grandmother, who wore them when she was Ann's age.

Ann is an intelligent, verbally rich woman, who quickly formed a very good rapport. She is articulate and insightful. At the end of the consultation process I offered her analysis, and she agreed enthusiastically to my offer, demonstrating a somewhat innocent, immediate trust.

Ann explained to me that her main concern was in the realm of forming close relationships, especially a romantic relationship with a man. She had had several intimate relationships, which she perceived as "frustrating, limited, and crippled." She was aware of the fact that she tended to choose men who were not available or not suitable for her and that she was not able to be authentic and spontaneous in these and other close relationships.

Ann described another pathological pattern in her life which she only vaguely understood. In the past few years, she continually created separations by moving on every two to three years. She usually enjoyed the first year in the new place and then her enthusiasm gradually diminished, and she started to feel a kind of deadness and developed an urge to pack her belongings and move on again. In one of the first sessions she told me, "I am like a street cat that has no home and gets along everywhere . . . or maybe I am more like a turtle whose home is always with him. I need only a small suitcase in which I can easily pack myself; several clothes, some books, my art creations and here I am on my way again."

Ann was aware of her ambivalent attitude towards separations. Although she created them all the time, they were actually very difficult for her. In the first few sessions she remembered that when she first left her home to live by herself, she suffered from psychosomatic symptoms, especially stomachaches. These symptoms recur every time she is about to leave. Ann wondered why she could not put down roots anywhere and create her own home. She felt that for her the only home was still her childhood home.

*

Ann described her mother as devoted and caring but felt the relationship was too close and "dangerously emotional." She felt that her mother had difficulty letting her go. Ann felt it was impossible to share emotional things with her mother. Whenever Ann was sad her mother became depressed, and whenever Ann was anxious her mother became panicky. Ann felt that there was no space between them and later in the treatment she named this situation "no membrane." Ann said that her mother has always suffered from existential anxiety and has had apocalyptic fantasies about death and loss. At the same time, Ann complained that there was no real closeness between them. Her mother was very passive, refrained from expressing her own ideas and feelings and was not really present in an authentic and lively way. Ann was always very sensitive to her mother's emotional responses and feelings, especially to her indirect, nonverbal messages, which were actually the main communicative channel between them.

134

Ann's father is a lawyer. He is a well-read person from whom Ann learned a lot. He was always willing to help her with any practical problem but was emotionally detached. He has had difficulty dealing with negative feelings and is easily hurt when criticized. When he feels offended, he tends to express a kind of restrained rage, which was always very frightening for Ann. She felt her relationship with him contributed to her own difficulty dealing with her anger and she has always tried to avoid conflicts in her relationships. Ann has a sister, four years her junior. She describes her sister as very demanding and angry and I have sensed that Ann often projects onto the image of her sister split-off parts of herself, which she cannot accept or contain.

*

With this initial information Ann and I embarked on the treatment. We started a once-a-week therapy and planned to move to a four times a week analysis on the couch, three months from then, when our schedules were going to allow it.

Ann's concerns over close relationships were expressed with me from the start, in the form of a wish–fear dilemma regarding starting an intensive therapy. On the one hand, she had many indirect associations about things that were not frequent enough, and talked about her need to have a firm structure and constant feedback in order to feel involved. On the other hand, when I suggested that she come twice a week, she refused and said she preferred to wait for the analysis. Her fantasies about the analysis seemed to be a compromise solution to her intimacy dilemma. She imagined that when she began using the couch she would not have to look at me and would be able to immerse herself in her internal world without having to relate or be influenced by me. The analysis symbolized clear and safe boundaries that could protect her from her fear of engulfment.

Around two months into the treatment, Ann met her current boyfriend. It was the first time that Ann had a real, stable relationship with a man. I wondered about the timing: was this a need to form a kind of triangle to defend against the dyadic relationship with me? Or was the relationship with me protecting her from engulfment with him? It seemed that in order to avoid being engulfed she had to form two close relationships at the same time.

In this way, Ann tried to create the conditions she needed to immerse herself in the treatment. Yet, when we started the four-times-a-week analysis the conflict intensified. Ann had difficulty modulating the level of closeness and reported that she felt as if she had no skin and everything was experienced as too intense. On her way to one of the first sessions she had an anxiety attack in the subway when the train was stuck in a tunnel.

In the small closed cabin in the subway car that had no open windows, she had a frightening thought about the sour air that everyone there was breathing. While listening to her, I became aware of the smallness of my office that had no windows and could feel for a moment a concordant claustrophobia: both of us trapped together in a too close, "emotionally dangerous" relationship, each of us inhaling the carbon dioxide that the other was exhaling. When I tried to make a comment about her fears, she experienced my interpretation as an unwelcomed intrusion and had a moment of anxiety again in the session. We were then able to talk about her fear that the relationship with me would be too close and intrusive and that she would not be able to find her space and freedom in it.

*

Gradually, Ann began to talk more about her difficulty expressing herself as a separate individual in my presence. She told me that she felt inhibited. It was difficult for her to initiate the sessions, to shift to another topic, and to be spontaneous. She remembered that it was always especially hard for her to express her feelings and needs with her mother. She began to talk about a discrepancy between what her mother said and her nonverbal communication and messages. Beneath her mother's tense silences Ann discerned unpleasant feelings and distress. She had to guess what her mother meant to say and tended to interpret everything the mother expressed as a sign of her disappointment. It was very difficult for Ann to have direct communication with her mother.

In our own moments of silence Ann felt a similar discomfort and told me that this had been present from the very first moment of the treatment. When I wondered out loud why Ann did not share with me this experience until now, Ann said, "I cannot even imagine myself telling you such a thing. It is so automatic for me to avoid talking directly about unpleasant experiences." She explained to me that as with her mother she feared I could get hurt by her or be disappointed with her.

During subsequent sessions we gradually explored this maternal transference and Ann realized that she was always worried that something bad would happen in our relationship if she expressed herself in my presence. Every moment of silence was an indication that there was something wrong and the relationship had been damaged. She was always very careful, as if she were walking on eggshells. When she initiated more active interactions, she felt as if she "intruded into my privacy" or "ate away" my existence. She told me that that is why she cancelled her own wants and needs in close relationships. "I totally lose myself in the relationship. Maybe that's why I am kind of autistic – I always escape to my aloneness," she added. I said to her: "It is as if you have only two available options: to be in a relationship where you renounce your needs, or to be alone. Maybe your wish in the treatment is to find a way to be together without losing yourself, to find your autonomy and freedom in the relationship." She later told me that this interpretation was very meaningful to her.

*

As a result of our initial work, Ann dared to express her wish to bring in some of her art creations, since "until now I kept my art outside of the treatment." She brought in one of her drawings that shed additional light on her core conflicts and defenses. In this drawing Ann is depicted as a piece of paper, which is being folded in the middle, divided into two symmetrical parts. Each part still has a leg and a hand but her heart is being squashed. "I have only one heart," she said, "and it is painful." Her associations led to her experience of being torn between her two worlds. France, where her family lived, represented closeness, care, and warmth. She feels the need to go there every few months to "charge her batteries." In London, where she lived and studied when she drew this picture, "which was so cold," she felt very lonely and deprived of connectedness, but there she had her other world: her studies, her art, her true self. She felt that the two worlds could not be combined. While telling me this, she suddenly had an insight. She realized that it was impossible for her to develop herself near her mother and that she had to distance herself and go abroad in order to start exploring her internal world and to begin a meaningful process of personal development.

During that period, I tried to understand the nature of Ann's conflicts and defenses better, and to assess the level of her psychic structure. Ann's fears of engulfment, her difficulty modulating affect, and the sense of blurred boundaries between her and her mother suggested an intense and almost symbiotic relationship with the early mother. At the same time, her ability to talk about these subtle and complex internal processes in a very articulate and self-reflective way suggested a more developed and differentiated level of development. It seemed that, for some reason, she could not express her rich and creative self with her mother, as if expressing her individuated self might in some way destroy her mother. I wondered about the nature of this lifelong bond with her mother that now kept her from self-realization and intimate relations with others.

*

We began to understand more about the bond with her mother, and her need to protect her, through dreams she reported before one of her trips to France, five months into the analysis. Throughout the first year of the treatment, Ann had a characteristic way of responding to our separations. Her reaction usually began with detachment and withdrawal and a kind of emotional numbness. There was a sense of deadness in the sessions. She usually felt a vague feeling of distress, which she could not verbalize or connect in any way to the fact of the separation. She severed the links between affect and thought, her characteristic defense whenever she was overwhelmed.

Before that specific break, her dreams reflected extreme distress and anxiety. They were a series of nightmares about huge tidal waves that were threatening to drown her. In the dreams, there was always another person for whom she felt responsible and whom she tried to instruct how to dive beneath the waves. There was a sense of helplessness, despair, and frustration since the other person was very passive and did not manage to do it and they were both in great danger. As we explored the associations to the dreams, Ann started to talk about her fear of visiting her parents, whom she always felt she had to take care of. Her mother has been depressed. She flooded Ann with detailed descriptions about her bad mood, her bodily pains, and her pessimistic stories and apocalyptic fantasies about the future. Ann felt as if her mother got under her skin. She also got depressed whenever she listened to her mother, as if there were no boundaries between them, "no membrane."

This experience of lack of emotional boundaries, where the other's pain becomes hers, made her reflect on this tangled bond she had with her mother. She realized that she had distanced herself from her mother in a physical sense but had not managed to separate from her emotionally. She came to the following session very excited and told me about a dream she had had the previous night. In her dream she saw a young bird in a nest. The bird starts to fly high in the air but then realizes that she cannot go too far because there is a string connecting her to the nest. Ann's associations led to her intense and limiting relationship with her mother. She used a metaphor of an umbilical cord (the string), to explain how she and her mother were connected in a mysterious way and how things have been transmitted between them nonverbally and through this imaginary umbilical cord, creating a private language that only they understood. I said to her: "You wish to free yourself" and she responded: "Yes, but if I do so, will I survive?" We talked about this dual experience of the bond with her mother that limited her freedom but was also life-sustaining.

Ann's growing ability to symbolize her relationship with her mother led to further insights into the nature of their bond, captured in another dream the following week. She dreamt about a young woman who needed psychological treatment. Ann gave the woman a chocolate bar and told her to break it into two parts. The woman, who was very attached to that chocolate bar, was reluctant to do it, and Ann forced her since it was the only way to help her. The woman cried and said that her mother did not allow her to do so. Ann added that actually in the dream the bar was already broken. She could feel the two separate parts through the wrapper that was still holding the two parts together.

The main theme in her associations was the difficulty she was experiencing in treatment. She felt that her attitudes were changing. She talked mainly about the change in the way she saw her mother. She started seeing negative aspects in their relationship. "It is difficult to criticize something that is part of you, values and attitudes on which you were raised," she said to me guiltily. I related this to the sense of loss in the dream, the fear that her negative feelings would destroy something precious. Ann agreed and added: "But actually the chocolate bar is already broken. Maybe I just have to acknowledge and accept something that already happened."

I was taken with the rich image of the chocolate bar. It confirmed my sense that Ann felt secretly separate from her mother but still wrapped together; she was not allowed to admit or announce their separateness. As she was progressing in the treatment towards accepting her separateness, she felt guilty about this "betrayal."

The chocolate-bar metaphor seemed to convey the essence of Ann's core object relationship in a condensed and rich way. As the treatment progressed, this metaphor grew richer, revealing more meanings that were gradually unfolding in the treatment. It also became a kind of touchstone, as I recalled it each time I understood something new about Ann and could see how it was represented in this condensed and creative image.

Over time, as Ann continued to talk about this complicated maternal bond, one that she tended to recreate in all her close relationships, I became aware of its actualization in our relationship as well, a nonverbal facet of the transference–countertransference that usually preceded understanding and symbolizing. During this period, which lasted a few months, I realized that I was constantly feeling uncomfortable about my interventions. On one hand, I felt that I was pushed to be active and say a lot because Ann was passive and laconic, but, at the same time, I felt I was too active and sensed that my interventions were too intense or too intrusive. I found myself trying to tone down my voice or to slow it down in order not to overwhelm her. Ann usually agreed with my interpretations and even added associations, but I was not sure whether it was an authentic participation or her way of adjusting herself to me. She is extremely sensitive, and usually a single word of mine was enough for her to understand my whole perspective, which she too easily adopted. On several occasions, after I said something, she stayed silent for a long time and then explained that my interpretation was too accurate and left her speechless. In such moments I felt as if I robbed her of her own ideas or feelings. It felt impossible to find a good place to be. It seemed that Ann had managed to draw me into that chocolate-bar wrapper with her and through this projective identification I could feel her fear of expressing her separateness and being herself. Like her, I felt that expressing myself freely could hurt the other's feelings or damage the relationship. Through this identification with her experience I began to be able to understand it more deeply and put it into words for her.

As I did so, Ann began to verbalize similar themes in all her close relationships, especially with her boyfriend. She talked about this entangled dyad of two people who are afraid to act as individuated individuals, because any one's act affected the other too intensely. The process of making any decision together became exhausting, because each person tried to guess what the other person liked to do and then comply. The result was a total paralysis in the relationship exactly as it was in her relationship with her mother. She brought up another image to explain her experience in close relationships. She felt as if the other person was the container and she was a kind of fluid that always took the shape of the container. She was afraid to be the solid container since then she would force the other person to take her shape. She started to realize that something here in the treatment reminded her of this frustrating and impossible atmosphere she had with her mother.

*

As she reflected on this kind of entangled relationship, she gradually began to react to my existence as a separate being. These moments occurred especially when I made a change in the setting; for example, I once had to cancel a session on short notice because of a snowstorm, revealing that I live out of town. Ann's reactions to these events were very charged and complex. On the more superficial level, she felt relief and even joy. She told me that the fact that I could express my own needs and assert myself enabled her to express hers and be more comfortable with herself. At the same time, on a deeper level, these occasions stirred up a lot of anxiety that was reflected in a series of anxiety dreams about the treatment. In these dreams there was a disruption of the treatment and everything went wrong. In one dream, we were sitting in a corridor with no privacy. I almost fell asleep in the middle of our session and was not available. In another, she dreamt that I had a baby who was screaming and Ann had to soothe her but did not manage to do so. When I directed Ann's attention to the anxiety, Ann said, "I have this feeling that when I think of you outside this room, our togetherness becomes impossible. Knowing something about you undermines my attempts to ignore that you have a life of your own." She added that whenever she saw my needs, she felt an immediate need to protect me and our relationship.

In the following sessions, Ann became more aware of this need to protect the other. She reflected again on the relationship with her mother and asked herself and me, "What is it that I have to protect her from?"

140

In the following week she tried to get an answer to that troubling question by initiating a series of conversations with her mother. For the first time she dared to share with her mother her frustration in their relationship. She talked with her about their shared passivity, both of them walking on eggshells, trying to protect the other all the time. Her mother's response was surprising for both of us. The mother began to talk about her history as a daughter of Holocaust survivors. It was the first time in the nine months of treatment that Ann talked about her family's Holocaust history. She told me that her mother's parents escaped to France before the Second World War. They both lost both parents, who were probably killed by the Nazis. Ann's mother explained to her that maybe that is why she was always fearful that the family will fall apart and felt a constant need to protect everyone from bad things. I suggested to Ann that maybe she absorbed the unspoken message that negative feelings could destroy and endanger relationships. In that session, Ann dared for the first time to express anger towards her mother about burdening her with her own traumas. Her mother's parents never spoke about the Holocaust, and her mother brought this unspoken and unspeakable loss and terror to her own family. Ann told me that as a child she had been obsessed with reading books and watching films about the Holocaust. She never knew why she was so attracted to this subject and never connected it to her own life. Now she understood that through the books she was trying to give words to her own personal holocaust. Her holocaust involved a lack of meaning, lack of words, feelings without content, horror without a story.

The discovery of her traumatic history shed light on many of Ann's issues: her intense sensitivity to her mother's distresses and her need to protect her; her sense of so many unspoken issues that she could not understand; her sensitivity to issues of separation and loss; her developmental guilt about having her own life; and her anxiety about expressing negative feelings, which she perceived as dangerous and destructive. The story of the Holocaust added a new dimension to the chocolate-bar image. Suddenly I had a picture of two people hiding together in the war, keeping their independence underground, hidden from the enemy. I thought again about Ann's relationship with her mother. Most probably every expression of Ann's separateness and the mundane small losses of a normal separation process between a mother and child were unbearable for Ann's mother as they stirred up the terrible separations, loss, and unresolved mourning of her own parents. I shared these insights with Ann.

*

During this period, around a year into the treatment, the issues of separation and separateness took center stage in the treatment. Whereas in previous breaks from the treatment Ann expressed overwhelming, diffuse distress that she could not verbalize or connect in any way to our separation, during this period, this wordless experience was gradually filled in with content: memories, fantasies, and more differentiated feelings.

She remembered that during her childhood, separations always stirred up fantasies about death and loss or feelings of abandonment and guilt. She realized that she typically "emptied" her relationships a long time before she was going to leave. Now she became aware that she was doing the same with me before our breaks, trying to turn our relationship into an unimportant one to make it easier to leave. "It is unbearable to miss something that you cannot have," she told me, when she realized with some pain that our relationship has really become important to her. "It is the first time I am forming really meaningful relationships, with my boyfriend and here in the analysis." She could not as yet say "with you."

Ann now began to explore her need to create separations all the time and to live far away from her family and friends. She remembered that her parents had the same need to distance themselves from their own parents, both physically and emotionally. She speculated that they needed to escape from the unbearable atmosphere they absorbed in their post-traumatic environment. Ann added that by avoiding the trauma and by refraining from working it through, they paradoxically recreated the same atmosphere in their own family, from which she now needed to distance herself. Indigestible nonverbal terror, unbearable pain, and apocalyptic fantasies were always in the air.

Ann felt she has been "recreating" her family history all her life, and began to explore the original trauma of her grandparents that had been unconsciously transmitted through the generations. Each of her maternal grandparents lost both their parents in the Holocaust. Her paternal grandparents did not lose their loved ones but they suffered other kinds of losses when they escaped to France. They lost property, status, and a sense of belonging, and experienced uncertainty, estrangement, and identity confusion. Her paternal grandfather had artistic talents which he gave up. He never adjusted to living in France and suffered a deep narcissistic injury from being expelled from his homeland.

*

Ann's associations led us to her art, and she asked me to look at some paintings she brought in. I was astonished to see the enormous impact this central conflict had on her art. The main theme in all the paintings was leaving, moving, and searching for a home that could never be reached. In several of them, you could see an old, funny-looking man, wearing old-fashioned clothes and holding an old worn-out suitcase. The man looks as if he is walking on a seemingly endless journey. Another group of paintings centered around a lone figure lying on a raft, floating in the middle of the ocean, looking frightened and confused. The atmosphere in all these paintings is one of total loneliness and estrangement. Ann told me that while working on these creations in London she did not have the slightest idea that it was connected to her own history, but she now realized that maybe it was her own identification with the story of her paternal grandfather. As a child, everyone in the family told Ann how much she resembled this grandfather and she was seen as his successor.

I said to her, "You carry within yourself the history of the family, the unbearable unspoken experiences that you absorbed, and you unconsciously tell these stories over and over again." I reflected on her need to be the "wandering Jew." Her solution to her personal holocaust was a compromise formation between her need to save her family on the one hand and her need to renounce that role on the other, between her need to escape the transmitted trauma as well as the need to relive it again and again.

*

Gradually, as we moved into the second year of the analysis, the fruits of our work were reflected in Ann's becoming more separate and more expressive while her clothing and appearance became less eccentric. I thought to myself that maybe she was able to give up the external proofs of her uniqueness, now that she was developing a clearer sense of autonomy. I noticed a new autonomy in her relationship with her mother, with her boyfriend, and with me. During that period Ann's mother was again depressed and panicky after Ann's sister got married and moved to another town. The mother was overwhelmed and reacted in her "Holocaustic" way (Ann's expression) as if it were a disaster, and had "no membrane" when she shared with Ann her unbearable distress. But this time, Ann was able to set emotional boundaries and was not consumed by the mother's distress. She confronted her mother and explained to her that she needed to distance herself in order not to get depressed too. She said to her mother, "I am not willing to sacrifice myself. I need to protect myself." She also told her mother that "getting married is not a disaster. It is actually a happy thing." In sessions she expressed a wish to renounce her special role with her mother and said humorously that she wanted to "divorce her mother" but was afraid to do so until she could find a substitute, who would be willing to listen to the mother's distresses.

Ann also started to express her need for boundaries and space within the treatment. In one session, after I commented about her need for boundaries and her fear of setting boundaries in a more direct way, she stayed silent for the last ten minutes of the session. I felt it was important not to interrupt the silence. I felt she was starting to signal her boundaries with me, showing the first signs of being able to be alone in my presence.

In subsequent sessions, there were many moments of silence when Ann chose to be alone. She also set boundaries by telling me when she wanted to change the subject or wanted to stop talking about something that was too distressing for her. There were several instances in which she expressed anger with me when she felt that my interventions forced her to deal with the emotional meaning of something when she still needed to deny or ignore it. I felt it was important not to interpret these reactions as resistance since I saw them as precious buds of autonomy.

*

During the second year of the analysis, our focus moved to Ann's wishes and fears regarding closeness and togetherness. She told me that in her family there was no real intimacy and the relationships were kind of shallow. From very early on, she got used to automatically warding off intense feelings and wishes. She realized that her current relationships were also shallow and unsatisfactory. She became aware of a wish to really give herself in the analysis and expressed pain and frustration about not being able to do it.

I became aware of sharp fluctuations from session to session. On occasion, she would suddenly begin to talk in a more direct way about her feelings and about the transference and then, after these more intimate sessions, she became detached and withdrawn again, severing the links between affect and thought. These estranged sessions threw some light on Ann's fears of intimacy which had to do with primitive oral fantasies about intrusion, engulfment, and fusion. She talked about these fears in a concrete way. She told me about her various somatic symptoms like stomachaches and mysterious viruses that infiltrated her body and disrupted her ability to function. She gradually realized that these fantasies came to her mind after intense interactions with people with whom she was close. In her fantasy, close interactions with her intrusive and demanding objects were experienced as if a foreign body intruded into her and disrupted everything from within. We could then better understand an eating ritual that we had discussed many times before. Every couple of months she goes on a severe diet for several weeks. Now, we connected it to her experience of being engaged in too close and overwhelming relationships with her mother, her boyfriend, and with me, the toxic effects of which she needed to empty herself, in order to regain a clearer sense of self.

During this period, especially in these estranged sessions, I also found it difficult to talk to Ann in a direct way, especially about our relationship. For example, in one of the sessions she mentioned a wish to move back to

Europe and shared with me some of her tentative plans. She did not mention her plans for the future (and the future of the treatment) again for a long time, and I did not raise the issue with her. I realized that I was colluding with her defenses and participating in a kind of an unspoken agreement not to talk directly about it. Sometimes I felt that when she talked about other relationships, we both knew that we were actually talking about our relationship, in a displaced way.

When I tried to direct Ann's attention to these issues, she tried to explain to me how she experienced our relationship. She said she did not experience me as a real object that existed outside her. She felt as if I was just reflecting back her own thoughts and feelings and the interactions between us were experienced as a kind of virtual dialogue within herself. "Maybe," she said, "I am afraid to see you as a real person and to see our relationship as a real, vivid, and significant one." She added that that is how she felt with her mother and commented that she felt as if her mother was always with us in the room. She had a dream that her boyfriend proposed to her and showed her a plastic dog that he was carrying around. She commented that dogs for her were symbols of attachment but in their relationship the attachment did not always feel real. She expressed frustration and despair about being stuck in this plastic and unreal kind of experience.

I began to look at the chocolate-bar image from another angle. It was not just that Ann's *separateness* – symbolized by the two separate pieces of chocolate – was hidden and unacknowledged. She also hid her secret *attachment* to her mother – the fact that the two of them were inextricably and suffocatingly wrapped together, bound in a secret agreement not to speak, and even not to know, about the Holocaust trauma they were living out with each other. Now as this was actualized in the transference–countertransference relationship, we both felt the entangled bond and the intensity of the dilemma: the wish to break out of the wrapper and feel our connectedness as real and significant, as well as the resistance and fear to do so. I reflected on this style of attachment that was probably transmitted through the three generations. I could imagine how, after the unbearable loss that her grandmother had suffered, it was so frightening to get attached again, to take the risk to feel one's own neediness, and to love again. Maybe that was why Ann and her mother formed this compromise formation – to be secretly attached but not really attached, and at the same time to be secretly separate but not fully separate.

Ann's frustration about being imprisoned in the analysis and within herself grew from session to session and I began to feel a little frustrated and impatient too. In one of these sessions, I found myself making a very long interpretation, telling Ann about my new insight and reminding her of the chocolate-bar dream, which she had already forgotten. I suggested to her that the avoidance of talking about the relationship has been recreated between us. I felt that I was less cautious than usual at that moment and that my tone of voice was much more passionate and emotional. Ann stayed silent and I became a little worried that I was overwhelming her, but, when the session ended, at the door, Ann looked directly into my eyes and said in an excited voice, "Thank you." It was a unique moment of a more direct interaction between us.

In the following session, Ann expressed feelings of joy and hope. She told me that when I talked in such an emotional way, she felt that I liberated her for a moment from this frustrating feeling of imprisonment. She said that she suddenly could feel me as a separate person who was very different from her mother. She could sense my personality and experienced our relationship at that moment as alive and real, one in which I really dared to express myself.

In the following week Ann was excited and seemed a little hypomanic. She had detailed and excited dreams. In one of them she gave birth to a baby daughter and in another she dreamt about both of us practicing gymnastics together and felt that we had a much more intimate kind of physical contact in the dream.

She also had many important insights about her relationship with her mother and about the prohibition against verbalizing conflicts and talking directly about their relationship. She realized that they had a kind of a secret language (a code) through which they communicated what was going on between them. She gave me an example of such a dialogue. She recently wondered why her mother had not answered her letters in a while and was worried that her mother was angry with her about her decision not to go back to France yet. She called her mother and asked her how the weather in France was. Her mother responded in a cold voice that the weather was bad and complained about a terrible headache. Ann felt that they were actually talking about the atmosphere between them. The real conversation went something like: Ann: "I feel guilty about wanting to stay in the States. How do you feel about it? Are you OK?" Her mother answers: "I am sad. It is painful." Her description also accurately reflected our mode of communication over the prior few months. I felt that we had also been talking in code.

It seemed that this kind of relationship protected Ann and her mother from the "dangerously emotional relationship" they both feared. We gained a better understanding about these primitive fears of closeness through a 19th-century story that Ann had read. She brought this story to a session without really knowing what she was trying to communicate. The story was about women vampires who formed intimate, erotic kinds of bonds. The narrator is a young woman who was a victim of the beautiful woman vampire. Gradually and patiently, the vampire tempted her into a love relationship and would secretly bite her on her breast while she was asleep.

146

Every bite made the victim more ill, since in this process the illness of the vampire was transmitted to her. The illness was a kind of depression since the woman's vitality was sucked out by the woman vampire. The victim was about to die and to turn into a vampire herself, as it had always happened in the previous generations of the vampires, but this time the woman was saved, at the last moment, by her father.

I thought it was a beautiful metaphor for the way the Holocaust trauma was transmitted through the generations of Ann's family. Through merger and love and in Ann's fantasy maybe through the incorporation of mother's milk – the bites were on the breast – the trauma was transmitted to the next generation, creating a new agent to carry the trauma forward. In Ann's unconscious, it was dangerous to love because love was poisonous and deadly.

We talked about Ann's fears of closeness that were reflected in this story. Ann told me that when she gets close to another person, an open channel is formed between the two people and things are transmitted between them without her being able to choose what to take in and what to leave out. She was afraid that she would absorb bad things that belonged to the other person or that good things would be drained out of her. That was how it was with her mother, who projected into her the unbearable trauma and also robbed her of her vitality when she (the mother) was depressed. She used a metaphor about breathing saying: "You cannot choose to take in just the oxygen and leave out the carbon dioxide." She smiled when she commented that we were also sitting together in a closed room with no windows, breathing the same air. I felt that this time the anxiety about our relationship was less overwhelming and Ann could relate to it with a sense of humor.

*

More recently, Ann began talking in a more direct way about our relationship. She had a fantasy of coming to a session and saying to me in a direct way, "Michal, let's talk about us." She started very hesitantly to express her own wishes as well as the variety of emotions that the relationship with me stirs up in her: dependency needs and longings, wishes for autonomy and for closeness, sadness, anxiety, and anger. She has become more present and lively and the dissociative states and moments of traumatic affect have become less frequent and less intense.

In one session she compared herself to a snail who dared to take his head out and see the world. She felt she was coming out of the "prison" and said she could not understand how she avoided relating to me in a more direct way for such a long time and how she refused to perceive our relationship as a personal one.

We are now in a really exciting period. She seems to be emerging from the confines of the wrapper and discovering me, a real object outside her, who she can desire. Or maybe it is more accurate to say that we have both emerged from our transference–countertransference wrapper, and have begun to be able to talk more directly about our relationship.

*

I would like to share with you one last aspect of the work with Ann. Throughout the process of writing this case, I found it hard to share the experience with my imaginary readers. I struggled with many dilemmas: how would I be able to describe this complex and intuitive process and put into words this unique experience that has to such a large degree been nonverbal? I reflected on my resistance to sharing my story with a third party and realized how it reflected once more the chocolate-bar image. I felt that Ann and I were wrapped together in our intense transference–countertransference relationship: needing to hide our togetherness from the world, at times perceiving any third party as the enemy. But at the same time, in Ann's story about the vampires, the third person is the savior. In her fantasy the father takes her out of the dangerous fusion with the mother. Maybe the analysis itself is a kind of a third, and the process of analyzing and verbalizing the "un-thought known" was what helped her to hatch from this disabling symbiosis and to consolidate her own autonomy and develop more capacity for intimacy.

Discussion

The treatment of Ann, so beautifully described by Michal Talby-Abarbanel, illustrates how aspects of unspeakable trauma – trauma that must be dissociated because it cannot be symbolized in words – can be passed on, unconsciously, from generation to generation. In this discussion, I will try to illustrate the particular nature of Ann's trauma, the dissociation evident in her psychic makeup, and the ways in which her unmetabolized, unverbalizable Holocaust trauma gained representation and expression through alternate channels: her lifelong somatic symptoms and behavioral patterns, her many artistic creations and, within her analysis, in the enacted dimension of the transference–countertransference matrix.

Trauma in Action: The Enacted Dimension of Analytic Process in a Third-Generation Holocaust Survivor

As Talby-Abarbanel described, a striking feature of the early work with Ann was her frequent states of traumatic affect that she could not process or digest. Ann would feel flooded and overwhelmed by unnamed and unnameable affects in one session, followed in the very next session by pervasive emotional numbness and detached ideation. To Talby-Abarbanel, these detached thoughts, by virtue of their content, were clearly related to the intense affect of the previous session. Ann, however, experienced no connection. The nature of this splitting and dissociation became understandable only much later, nearly nine months into the treatment, when the material emerged about the annihilation of much of her mother's extended family, and the dislocation of much of her father's extended family, in the Holocaust. Because the emotional sequelae of these devastating traumas were transmitted from generation to generation – from her grandparents, to her parents, to Ann – without ever being put into words, the unmetabolized emotional experiences became sequestered and completely dissociated from Ann's otherwise intact symbolizing capacities. Unable to be accessed on the verbally symbolic level, the family Holocaust trauma was, instead, encoded and expressed on the sensorimotor level: in Ann's unmetabolized affect states, her somatic symptoms, and her eating rituals – and, more globally, in her propensity to live her life as a "wandering Jew," her near-compulsive need to move to a different country every couple of years. These modes of experiencing and regulating the trauma organized virtually every aspect of her functioning, influencing relationships and decisions, large and small, in her daily life.

The split-off experience of her family's Holocaust trauma was also represented and expressed, throughout Ann's life, and without any conscious awareness, in her paintings and her many artistic creations. These became a key feature of her analysis as well: drawings, paintings, and stories, all supplemented Ann's equally rich dreams and associative images and metaphors. The treatment was a veritable multimedia presentation. Being blessed with artistic talent from birth provided Ann with a channel for the expression of the unsymbolizable experiences she was forced to carry, and they no doubt saved her from more severe psychological disruption in her development. And, equally fortunate for Ann, was finding Talby-Abarbanel, an analyst who could understand these dissociated symbols, tolerate her psychic split and emotional dilemma, and then, with enormous empathy and sensitivity, enable her gradually to come to terms with her world and begin a process of integration and repair.

A third, powerful, way the dissociated aspects of the trauma found symbolic representation in the treatment was in the nonverbal, enacted dimension of the transference–countertransference matrix. What found symbolic actualization was both the dissociated and unsymbolized existential anxieties of the Holocaust, as well as the nonverbal and unacknowledged arrangement with her mother that maintained the dissociation. From the treatment's inception, and for the better part of the treatment to the date reported, this powerful, nonverbal aspect of the analytic relationship formed its continuous backdrop – but again, it was only understandable much later, in retrospect. As described by Talby-Abarbanel, it constituted the essence of those long and intense periods in the treatment in which patient and analyst literally felt enveloped in that chocolate-bar wrapper – secretly attached and secretly separate – a tortured relationship, or, to use Ann's phrase, an "emotionally dangerous" relationship, that neither wanted to be in but from which neither could leave. Before the material about the Holocaust emerged – that is, before Talby-Abarbanel could have any clear idea what this transference–countertransference configuration was about – there were those long periods, as Talby-Abarbanel reported, in which both felt like they were walking on eggshells with each other – Ann fearful that any expression of her autonomous self would destroy her analyst, and her analyst fearful that any intervention, or any nonintervention, would destroy the treatment. So sealed in their wrapper were they that, at moments, Talby-Abarbanel actually felt Ann's unformulated, inchoate terror and could not be sure from whom, or from where, this experience originated – there was "no membrane," again to use Ann's phrase. As Ann and her mother had long done, Talby-Abarbanel also found herself speaking with Ann in code, not talking about the real thing or else talking in displaced arenas, both of them fully knowing, but never acknowledging, what they were really talking about. And even after the material about the Holocaust finally began to emerge, Talby-Abarbanel found herself feeling that discussion of any experience of attachment and loss – particularly as experienced in the analytic relationship – was inadmissible, a dangerous and forbidden subject in the analysis, the same taboo under which three generations of Holocaust survivors had suffered.

This recreation in the transference–countertransference was abruptly shattered when Talby-Abarbanel, without conscious planning, suddenly found herself putting into words for Ann – in one lengthy, powerful intervention and with, what was for her she tells us, an atypical degree of intensity and comprehensiveness – everything she had actually come to understand for a while, but from her position within the transference–countertransference wrapper could not previously utter. Talby-Abarbanel states that she worried about her unusual intervention, but she could also see that she felt freed and more alive – it was as if the allied forces had suddenly liberated the camps and a new world became visible and possible. I see Talby-Abarbanel's intervention as part and parcel of the enacted process, a response to what was likely Ann's communication, both conscious and unconscious, that she was ready to emerge from the maternal transference–countertransference wrapper both had been in for nearly a year and a half, and to begin the process of bearing witness to and integrating – integrating, rather than dissociating – this aspect of her psychic heritage

150

and coming to terms with it as best she might. Through this enacted process, Ann was afforded the opportunity to convert what had been passively experienced in childhood into something that was actively (even if unconsciously) intended and which, through this "new edition," could now be actively mastered. To return to the theoretical point I made in Chapter 7 about "co-creation": while the particular shape of this new analyst–patient interaction was co-created by the analytic pair, Ann's transference issues and Talby-Abarbanel's countertransference issues were unique to their individual history and internal dynamics.

This entire process – the creation, and the analysis, of the new edition of the trauma in the enacted dimension of the transference–countertransference matrix – was thus a necessary transitional state that allowed the dissociated trauma to achieve a higher level of symbolic representation and thereby become available for analytic consideration and working through. It was also a *formative* psychic activity. It was an analytic process in which new psychic representations were constructed as Ann's dissociated ego states were gradually integrated rather than an analytic process characterized by a lifting of repression and the recall of a once conscious representational memory. That aspect of analytic treatment of patients with such severe, dissociated trauma – the working through of the many layers of conflict, defense, and psychic meaning that subsequently became attached to the trauma and part of the her personality structure – only begins to be possible at this point.

A final word about Ann's analyst. In addition to her analytic fortitude and commitment to her patient, Talby-Abarbanel brought to this analysis a well-developed capacity and talent for using her *self* – her own fantasies, reveries, and emotional states – in the service of understanding her patient. Her capacity to oscillate between, on the one hand, an immediate, intense, and direct identification with her patient and, on the other hand, a differentiated state of observation and analytic assessment – evident in her presentation – was a key ingredient in the creation, sustaining, and ultimate emergence from the enacted maternal transference. These qualities enabled Talby-Abarbanel simultaneously to be a participant in the undifferentiated wrapper experience – going to the edge, even, at moments, a bit over the edge – and also to be a separate, differentiated self, one with which Ann could ultimately identify. I have been privileged to discuss her work.

Note

1 The case of Ann, and my discussion, were originally published in *A New Freudian Synthesis: Clinical Process in the Next Generation*, edited by Andrew B. Druck, Carolyn Ellman, Norbert Freedman, and Aaron Thaler, London: Karnac Books, 2011, Chapter 10, pp. 219–247.

Part IV

FREQUENTLY ASKED QUESTIONS (AND ANSWERS)

In this final part, I address a few issues that did not find an organic place in the body of the book. For the most part, however, my purpose here is different. Over the course of teaching seminars and presenting papers on enactment, I have found that I am regularly asked very similar kinds of questions. While the various chapters of this book do address these questions, I have come to the conclusion that they arise so frequently because they reflect issues that are more easily digested when approached more than once, and from different directions. It is thus my hope that these questions and answers will provide a useful review and working through of the central ideas presented in this book.

FREQUENTLY ASKED QUESTIONS (AND ANSWERS)

1. Is enactment entirely a process between two minds, or does it also say something about one mind?

As I discussed in Chapter 7 with regard to the various theoretical concepts that emphasize the interaction between two minds (interpsychic interaction, interpersonal interaction, intersubjectivity, the analytic third, and co-creation) – enactment is a process that concerns two minds *and* one mind *at the same time.* In psychoanalytic treatment, two one-person intrapsychic realities meet in a two-person, interactive field. The intrapsychic and the interactive (which is composed of interpsychic, interpersonal, and intersubjective elements) are different aspects of, or different perspectives on, the same process and the same data. In the enacted dimension, both a transference and a countertransference issue (a conflict, a fantasy, a defense, a traumatic early object-relationship, etc.), stimulated by the interpsychic interpenetration of each participant's unique psychic organization, become actualized through interactive action (motor action or verbal action). This action is an unconscious creation of *both* minds and is thus unique to that patient–analyst dyad. Again, it is useful to think of an enacted process as a two-party waking dream taking place in the room: the unconscious issue in each psyche is its latent content; the co-constructed action is the manifest content that serves to actualize the two sets of unconscious issues.

2. Even with the understanding that enactment is an interactive transference–countertransference process, could one still distinguish between a primarily transference enactment and a primarily countertransference enactment?

We are now more fully aware of the fact that both transference and countertransference (the unconscious components of the patient's and the analyst's subjectivities) find expression not only through words but also through action. As such, we can speak of the enacted *dimension* of transference, and we can speak of the enacted *dimension* of countertransference. However, this fuller, more accurate, under- standing of transference and countertransference, as important as it is, does not really address unconscious enacted *interactions* within the transference–countertransference matrix – the interpsychic processes that comprise the enacted dimension of analytic process. I would there- fore restrict the term "enactment," or "enacted process," to this aspect of analytic treatment. In such a process, which is a continuous one, place of origin and quantitative questions – whether they arose solely, or more, from the patient or solely, or more, from the analyst – are not as important as the analytic use to which they are put. Regardless of whether the analyst's (or the patient's) part is large or small, the primary treatment focus is on what was unconsciously experienced by the patient, the unconscious fantasy or experience that it came to actualize.

3. Is it possible to say when an enacted process begins? Is it important to do so?

As with the question of "who" initiated it, the question of "when" it started is also not particularly relevant. The enacted dimension is con- tinuously and dynamically evolving. The unconscious interpsychic interactions that underlie the process begin in the very first meeting. It is what accounts for what we commonly refer to as a good (or bad) patient–analyst "match" or "chemistry." It is the unconscious reason, underlying the various concrete, conscious reasons, a patient feels a con- nection with and chooses one analyst over another after a series of con- sultations. I think a patient needs to have an unconscious sense that the analyst is similar enough to the original object so that he or she can recreate the relationship and conflicts in the treatment, yet also dif- ferent enough from the original object so that something new can happen. This forms the basis of what then transpires in the enacted dimension. Looking back at the Sandler and Renik vignettes in Chapter 5, for example, it is likely that both patients had unconsciously sensed an issue in their respective analysts that could fulfill this "some- thing old, something new" paradigm, something that, in each case, would enable a recreation of the original traumatic relationship with the mother, and then something that would enable a new experience of the old trauma thereby providing a genuine, spontaneous corrective experience.

Unconscious interpsychic interaction resulting in the actualization of an unconscious fantasy or a dissociated experience can even begin *before* the first appointment, during the phone contact that arranges the consultation. To illustrate: I had a patient who called for a consultation session saying that he was currently in an analysis that had to end (the analyst was retiring and moving away) and asked if I had time on a particular Monday about a month away. I told him I did, and also asked when the current analysis was ending. He said his last session was scheduled for the Friday before that Monday. I asked him if he had thought about the possibility of taking some time between treatments. He said he preferred to start right away, and so we made the appointment.

What we learned, in bits and pieces over many, many months, was that the patient's biological father left the family when he was about 15 months old and was immediately replaced by a stepfather. (The parents divorced and the mother immediately married the man with whom she was having an affair.) The mother and stepfather, for various conscious and unconscious reasons, had no conception that my patient could possibly have any reactions or that there could possibly be any repercussions to this event. He was "too young" they told themselves, and him, and convinced themselves – and communicated to him – that his life began with the new family unit. His curiosity and questions after he learned of the events during his latency years were brushed off: "There's nothing more to know – it doesn't matter." The patient was always very close to his mother; his stepfather was a narcissistic, self-important bully who competed with him and consistently tried to crush him. He grew up to be shy, passively compliant, and quite timid.

What this patient thus succeeded in recreating – even before we ever met – was the traumatic, preverbally experienced, emotional dislocation I have described. The first analyst and treatment had been idealized, as he had idealized his biological father in fantasy, and he unconsciously positioned me to be instantaneously experienced as a confusing and terrifying new presence, as he had experienced his stepfather. All of this took place enactively, without verbal symbolization, so it took quite a bit of time to realize just how terrified he was of me. His fear took the form of inchoate physiological and psychological states – rapidly racing heartbeat, inaccessible unformed thoughts, and intense and diffuse panic states – but it was all initially hidden beneath his very compliant and pleasant demeanor.

The "something old, something new" paradigm in that initial phone call was as follows: my response to the way he wanted to proceed had been to ask more about it, but also not to press him on it or make it an

157

issue. (While this particular intervention might be one most analysts would make, it was also an outgrowth of a personal sensitivity to issues of early object loss.) I believe that my communication – that we could begin but that there was something more to be understood about his request – had unconsciously assured him that something old and something new could happen in this treatment. It assured him that his early preverbal experience would not only be actualized, but that *this* time questions about what had happened *would* be permitted. As this gradually unfolded and became conscious over the course of the analysis, he was slowly able to verbally symbolize the new treatment edition of his early formative event, and reintegrate his previously forbidden reactions and feelings with a gradually internalized new therapeutic object.

4. **Regarding the Sandler vignette, what would have happened had the patient had a different analyst who was not inclined to pass the tissue box?**

The content of any treatment is determined primarily (although not exclusively) by the content and force of the patient's unconscious conflicts. The particular *form* the treatment takes – that is, which of the patient's issues emerge when, and the manner in which they get verbally expressed or enactively actualized – is determined primarily (although not exclusively) by the interactive mix with the subjectivity of the particular analyst. While there are many things about Sandler's reactions to his patient that we do not know (the paper was written in 1976, long before it became customary, even obligatory, to disclose one's countertransference in published reports), we can surmise that something in Sandler's history and unconscious conflictual life made him particularly reactive to this patient's tears, and made him susceptible to be enlisted in a caretaking enactment. The patient may well have unconsciously sensed her analyst's vulnerabilities the first time she cried and utilized this to actualize her early trauma. Had she had a different analyst, with a different set of dynamics, I believe her internal need to actualize the trauma would have found a different quality in her analyst or the analytic environment (a different manifest content to use the dream analogy) with which to do so – perhaps a particular positive way the analyst responded emotionally to her (as the patient in the Renik vignette utilized during the first period of work in that enacted process), or some other verbal or nonverbal hook. Remember, there does not have to be any unusual action or behavior on the part of the analyst for the patient to have the experience that an unconscious wish or fantasy is being actualized. A patient's unconscious is resourceful enough to utilize an aspect of any average-expectable analytic environment, or a characteristic of any good-enough analyst. It is then a matter of how the analyst and patient make analytic use of it as they become aware of it.

5. **What, if anything, gets lost or compromised when there is a big theoretical emphasis on enactment? Two examples might be the idea of resistance and the patient's unconscious fantasies.**

Neither of these things is sacrificed. Enacted processes *are* the manifestation (the actualization) of the patient's unconscious fantasies and resistances that have been brought to life in the here-and-now of the transference–countertransference matrix. Like a dream or symptom, they are compromise formations that include unconscious fantasies and wishes; early anxieties and defenses along with new adaptive solutions; and old object-relational experiences along with new experiences with a new object. While there may be currently "a big theoretical emphasis" on enactment due to the widespread interest in the interactive aspects of analytic process, in actual clinical practice it should not be emphasized any more than the other routes – dreams, fantasies, symptoms, etc. – for gaining understanding and insight into the patient's psyche.

6. **Is there any reason to use the term "acting out" anymore?**

The short answer is no. One doesn't really hear or see the term being used anymore. It has largely been replaced by the concept of enactment. The term "acting out" is a relic of Freud's early topographic model of the mind that understood action to be in opposition to remembering, rather than a way of remembering (see Chapter 1). Further, the term failed to distinguish the *actualization* of the underlying transference fantasies from the external motor behavior that accompanied it (Boesky, 1982; Laplanche & Pointalis, 1967). As a result, the term actually had the unfortunate effect of taking action out of the realm of psychoanalytic consideration. Trying to understand an "acting out" became like trying to understand a dream by considering just the manifest content, or focusing exclusively on the masturbatory act and ignoring the underlying fantasies.

7. **If enactments are constantly occurring, and if there can be many of them in a treatment, how does one determine when something is an enactment or which one to address?**

One doesn't have much choice about these things because the actualization processes that are taking place in the enacted dimension are largely unconscious. Remember John Lennon: enactments are what happen to you while you are doing psychoanalysis. As the process taking place in the enacted dimension does become available to conscious recognition, the analyst can then address it and analyze it as he or she would any other manifestation of unconscious process. This answer, however, should be taken as a general way of thinking about enactment and analytic technique. The answers to the next three questions address some fine points.

8. **When would you address an enacted process once you do become aware that it has taken place? Are there times when the analyst should exercise forbearance in pointing out and discussing an enactment that he or she perceives?**

When both patient and analyst become ready to accept into consciousness what had been previously unconscious or dissociated, discussing the enacted process then becomes a joint endeavor in the way the analyst and patient customarily analyze anything. This is the case, for instance, when a dissociated trauma's time frame has taken its course – like when Sandler failed to pass the tissue box or when Renik made his hostile interpretation. In both cases the participants were ready for the enacted recreation of the trauma to enter consciousness, and for both dimensions of the treatment to be integrated through interpretive work.

However, when the analyst recognizes something before the patient is emotionally available to consider it, the question of when and how to point it out falls under the general rubric of analytic timing and sensitivity. When the analyst tries to point out the observable aspect of an enacted process before the patient is ready, the underlying unconscious conflicts and issues will likely find another outlet, or simply persist in the same way. The treatment of Jimmy (Chapter 12) is a case in point.

To make matters more complicated, it is also important to keep in mind that enacted processes take place at different levels of consciousness simultaneously and serve multiple psychic functions. *The analytic couple will often be enacting the very object-relationship they are analyzing, and a "successful" analysis of an enacted process may also be an enactment of something else.* As an example of the more conscious kind of enacted process, most of us have probably had the following kind of experience: feeling a need to say something to a patient, consciously thinking that it shouldn't be said either because the timing is wrong or because the urgency of the impulse points to too much countertransference involvement, and then, simultaneously, hearing yourself speaking it anyway. On a slightly less conscious level, the analyst or the patient may have a vague idea that they are involved in some kind of enacted process but are unable to access it. Even with the more conscious or preconscious kinds of enactment, however, there are always aspects of the enacted dimension that remain out of awareness, and any enacted process may be defending against the actualization of a different set of unconscious conflicts.

9. Is verbal interpretation of enactment required or not?

Assuming the patient is also ready to consider what transpired and is emotionally available to work on it, what would be the harm? If the question is which is more important to the process of psychic change – insight via interpretation, or the experience in the relationship – I would say that the two should not be dichotomized or polarized. As I have emphasized and illustrated throughout this book: insight and experience operate together and potentiate each other. One needs insight in order to have new experiences (both inside and outside the treatment) and new experiences provide opportunities for new insight.

10. If enactment is an interactive or co-constructed process, does the analyst need to disclose more?

With regard to how to think about what, or what not, to "disclose" in an interactive enacted process, it is helpful to remember the distinction I made in Chapter 7 about what is, and what is not, co-constructed. From my perspective, neither the analyst's countertransference nor the patient's transference is co-constructed. I consider these to be separate entities, each the product of a unique psychic organization. What *is* co-constructed is a "third" thing – the particular form or shape aspects of the transference and countertransference have taken through their interpsychic interaction. Thus, I would certainly acknowledge, and if appropriate apologize for, my part in the *interaction* – "Yes, I have always passed the tissue box for you, and I don't know why I didn't do so this time." But I would not immediately discuss the details of what I understood about my countertransference because, at that point, it would not be likely that I understood very much about the *unconscious* issues that had contributed to my involvement in the enacted process. The fact that an enacted process has an interactive component, does not mean that the analyst necessarily "needs," in any *a priori* way, to disclose more about his or her part. This is not to say that it might not be advantageous for the analyst to do so at some point in the ongoing discussion of the enacted process if such disclosure would be useful to the process of elucidating what the enacted process unconsciously actualized in patient. Deliberate self-disclosure has its place, particularly at moments with more narcissistically vulnerable patients (see C. Ellman, 2011, for a recent discussion), but it is also a complex issue. The analyst would need to keep in mind how any disclosure might be part of a different enacted process that may be actualizing a different set of unconscious issues in either participant.

11. How does an appreciation of the enacted dimension affect supervisory technique? Would supervisory intervention interfere with the inevitable and necessary unfolding of the process?

Regarding the supervisory process in general, I consider one of its important tasks, among the many that comprise the supervisor's role and educational responsibility, to be fostering in the supervisee an interest in what may be transpiring in the enacted dimension of the treatment case. As a supervisor I try to make consideration of the many levels and avenues of interpsychic communication a central focus of how the supervisee and how I listen to the analytic (as well as the supervisory) material. To be clear, I am talking here about expanding the purview of analytic listening and consideration; I am not proposing the teaching of any kind of specific technical approach to enactment. As I indicated in Chapter 8, the enacted dimension is a descriptive part of analytic process and not a prescriptive component of technique, either by the analyst or by the supervisor.

That said, there will be occasions when the supervisor will be able to observe an enacted process and point it out, to therapeutic effect, to the supervisee. In these instances, however, it is likely that the enacted process became available in the supervisory process because it was already emerging into consciousness in the treatment process. But when the underlying issues need to *remain* unconscious or dissociated, they will find a way to do so even when the manifest level of the process is pointed out to the analyst in supervision (see also, Questions 8 and 10). Thus, had Sandler been in supervision during the case of "the tissue box enactment" (Chapter 5), and had his supervisor wondered aloud what might have been underlying the behavior, it would not have affected the *underlying unconscious* process unless both Sandler and his patient were ready for it to be affected. In this sense, the essential nature of enactment – which is the ongoing unconscious process – is not affected by a "supervisory intervention."

I would also point out that it is not a given that the supervisor, simply because he or she has a more objective perspective on the treatment process, will be able to recognize an enacted process before the supervisee. This is especially the case when the issue being enacted also has unconscious resonance for the supervisor. As in the two supervisory vignettes discussed in Chapter 9, the supervisor may well become part of a triadic enacted process. In other words, the factors that limit the analyst's awareness of, and ability to interpret, an enacted process may also limit the supervisor's awareness and ability to make a supervisory intervention. In the end, the main thing a supervisor does is instill in the supervisee a general awareness of the enacted dimension and an openness to its discovery.

12. Is the enacted dimension more common in cases of trauma – that is, in treatments where dissociation, as opposed to repression, is the major defense mechanism?

The enacted dimension is an ongoing component of every treatment process. Any experience that cannot be symbolized verbally – whether an early childhood experience or a contemporary one, whether traumatic in origin or whether psychically conflictual in origin – will nonetheless become represented in enactive memory (in neurobiological terms, encoded in the sensorimotor, subsymbolic brain centers) and, in treatment, will find expression in the enacted dimension. I don't think it is useful to make sharp distinctions between dissociated trauma and repressed unconscious conflict. The psychological issues we work with are complex, multiply determined, and layered mixtures of both. Trauma is better understood not simply as an environmental event, but as a particular interaction between the psyche and the environment. All of the developmental challenges and psychic conflicts of childhood will be experienced as more or less traumatic depending on the environmental context, and every trauma, early childhood or contemporary, will also be personally elaborated and colored by ongoing unconscious fantasies, meanings, and conflicting affects. This is not to minimize the significant differences among different kinds of trauma – the trauma of war combat, for example, is qualitatively different from that involved in childhood sexual abuse suffered in the context of an intimate relationship to a parent. Nor is it to minimize the fact that dissociation is a central defensive response to trauma and that extreme kinds of trauma will pose particular treatment issues and technical challenges. It is simply to say that there are a great many kinds of experiences that cannot, at the time of their occurrence, be emotionally integrated by the individual, that the kinds of defenses deployed against them are multiple and overdetermined, and that all unformulated experience will find expression and representation in the enacted dimension of the treatment through the interpsychic interaction that is unique to each patient–analyst dyad.

13. **Your last answer notwithstanding, aren't some enactments more enactment than others? In other words, wouldn't trauma and dissociation lead to greater amounts or specific kinds of enactment? Or have some special quality?**

These questions are reflections of the very problem that I have specifically tried to correct in this book – the mistaken focus on the overt/manifest/behavioral/action form taken by the un-verbally symbolizable issues, whatever they may be, however they were defended against. In a given case this manifest overt form may be more (or less) starkly visible, disruptive, behavioral, etc. – so yes, a particular kind of trauma may get *represented* by a greater amount, or a particular kind, or particular quality, of overt behavior or disruptive kind of interaction. But in my view the particular shape it takes is not what defines "enactment." Enactment is the *process* by which the underlying issues, conflicts and traumas find meaning and representation through the unique interpsychic interaction between the two participants. Enactment is process, not event. Enactment is the play within the play, the enacted dimension of every analytic process.

REFERENCES

Abend, S. M. (1989). Countertransference and psychoanalytic technique. *Psychoanalytic Quarterly, 58*, 374–95.

—— (1993). An inquiry into the fate of the transference in psychoanalysis. *Journal of the American Psychoanalytic Association, 41*, 627–51.

Altschul, S. (1968). Denial and ego arrest. *Journal of the American Psychoanalytic Association, 16*, 301–18.

Anthi, P. R. (1983). Reconstruction of preverbal experience. *Journal of the American Psychoanalytic Association, 31*, 33–59.

Arlow, J. (1963). The supervisory situation. *Journal of the American Psychoanalytic Association, 11*, 576–94.

Aron, L. (1996). *A Meeting of Minds: Mutuality in Psychoanalysis.* Hillsdale, NJ: The Analytic Press.

—— (2003). The paradoxical place of enactment in psychoanalysis: Introduction. *Psychoanalytic Dialogues, 13*, 623–31.

—— (2006). Analytic impasse and the third: Clinical implications of intersubjective theory. *International Journal of Psychoanalysis, 87*, 349–68.

Auerhahn, N. C. & Laub, D. (1998). The primal scene of atrocity: The dynamic interplay between knowledge and fantasy of the Holocaust in children of survivors. *Psychoanalytic Psychology, 15*, 360–77.

Bach, S. (1994). *The Language of Perversion and the Language of Love.* Northvale, NJ: Jason Aronson.

Bachant, J., Lynch, A. A., & Richards, A. D. (unpublished). The spectrum of analytic interaction: A contemporary Freudian perspective.

Bass, A. (2003). "E" enactments in psychoanalysis: Another medium, another message. *Psychoanalytic Dialogues, 13*, 657–75.

Baudry, F. (1993). The personal dimension and management of the supervisory situation with a special note on the parallel process. *Psychoanalytic Quarterly, 62*, 588–614.

Benjamin, J. (1988). *The Bonds of Love.* New York: Pantheon Books.

—— (1990). An outline of intersubjectivity: The development of recognition. *Psychoanalytic Psychology, 7*, 33–46.

—— (1992). Recognition and destruction: An outline of intersubjectivity. In N. Skolnick & S. C. Warsaw (Eds.), *Relational Perspective in Psychoanalysis* (pp. 43–60). Hillsdale, NJ: The Analytic Press.

—— (2010). Where's the gap and what's the difference? The relational view of intersubjectivity, multiple selves, and enactments. *Contemporary Psychoanalysis, 46*, 112–19.

Beren, P. (Chair) (1995). *Parallel Process and Supervision.* Panel presented at the Institute for Psychoanalytic Training and Research (IPTAR), March, New York, NY.

Berman, E. (2000). Psychoanalytic supervision: The intersubjective development. *International Journal of Psychoanalysis, 81*, 273–90.

Bion, W. (1959). Attacks on linking. *International Journal of Psychoanalysis, 40*, 308–15.

Black, M. J. (2003). Enactment: Analytic musings on energy, language, and personal growth. *Psychoanalytic Dialogues, 13*, 633–55.

Blos, P. (1979). *The Adolescent Passage: Developmental Issues.* New York: International Universities Press.

Blum, H. (1983). The splitting of the ego and its relation to parent loss. *Journal of the American Psychoanalytic Association, 31*, 301–24.

Boesky, D. (1982). Acting out: A reconsideration of the concept. *International Journal of Psychoanalysis, 63*, 39–55.

—— (1989). Enactments, acting out, and considerations of reality. Paper presented at the panel: *Enactments in Psychoanalysis*, American Psychoanalytic Association, San Francisco, CA.

—— (1990). The psychoanalytic process and its components. *Psychoanalytic Quarterly, 59*, 550–84.

—— (1995). Parallel process and supervision. Paper presented at the panel: *Parallel Process and Supervision*, the Institute for Psychoanalytic Training and Research (IPTAR), March, New York, NY.

—— (2000). Affect, language and communication: 41st IPA Congress Plenary Session. *International Journal of Psychoanalysis, 81*, 257–62.

Bollas, C. (2001). Freudian intersubjectivity: Commentary on paper by Julie Gerhardt and Annie Sweetnam. *Psychoanalytic Dialogues, 11*, 93–105.

Bolognini, S. (2011). *Secret Passages: The Theory and Technique of Interpsychic Relations* (trans. G. Atkinson). London and New York: Routledge.

Bowlby, J. (1969). *Attachment and Loss*, vol. I: *Attachment.* New York: Basic Books.

Bromberg, P. M. (2000). Potholes on the royal road: Or is it an abyss? *Contemporary Psychoanalysis, 36*, 5–28.

—— (2003). One need not be a house to be haunted: On enactment, dissociation, and the dread of "not-me" – A case study. *Psychoanalytic Dialogues, 13*, 689–709.

—— (2006). *Awakening the Dreamer: Clinical Journeys.* Mahwah, NJ: Analytic Press.

—— (2011). *The Shadow of the Tsunami and the Growth of the Relational Mind.* London and New York: Routledge.

Brown, L. J. & Miller, M. (2002). The triadic intersubjective matrix in supervision: The use of disclosure to work through painful affects. *International Journal of Psychoanalysis, 83*, 811–23.

Bucci, W. (1997). Symptoms and symbols: A multiple code theory of somatization. *Psychoanalytic Inquiry, 17*, 151–72.

—— (2001). Pathways of emotional communication. *Psychoanalytic Inquiry, 20*, 40–70.

—— (2007). Dissociation from the perspective of multiple code theory, Part I: Psychological roots and implications for psychoanalytic treatment. *Contemporary Psychoanalysis, 43*, 165–84.

—— (2011a). The interplay of subsymbolic and symbolic processes in psychoanalytic treatment: It takes two to tango – but who knows the steps, who's the leader? The choreography of the psychoanalytic interchange. *Psychoanalytic Dialogues, 21*, 45–54.

—— (2011b). The role of embodied communication in therapeutic change: A multiple code perspective. In W. Tschacher & C. Bergomi (Eds.), *The Implications of Embodiment: Cognition and Communication* (pp. 209–28). Exeter: Imprint Academic.

—— (2011c). The role of subjectivity and intersubjectivity in the reconstruction of dissociated schemas: Converging perspectives from psychoanalysis, cognitive science and affective neuroscience. *Psychoanalytic Psychology, 28*, 247–66.

Busch, F. (1989). The compulsion to repeat in action: A developmental perspective. *International Journal of Psychoanalysis, 70*, 535–44.

—— (1995). Do actions speak louder than words? A query into an enigma in analytic theory and technique. *Journal of the American Psychoanalytic Association, 43*, 61–82.

Caligor, L. (1981). Parallel and reciprocal processes in psychoanalytic supervision. *Contemporary Psychoanalysis, 17*, 1–27.

Casement, P. (1982). Some pressures on the analyst for physical contact during the re-living of an early trauma. *International Review of Psycho-Analysis, 9*, 279–86.

—— (2000). The issue of touch: A retrospective overview. *Psychoanalytic Inquiry, 20*, 160–84.

Chused, J. (1991). The evocative power of enactments. *Journal of the American Psychoanalytic Association, 39*, 615–39.

—— (1992). The patient's perception of the analyst: The hidden transference. *Psychoanalytic Quarterly, 61*, 161–84.

—— (1996). The therapeutic action of psychoanalysis: Abstinence and informative experiences. *Journal of the American Psychoanalytic Association, 44*, 1047–71.

—— (1997). Discussion of "Observing-participation, mutual enactment, and the new classical models." *Contemporary Psychoanalysis, 33*, 263–77.

—— (2003). The role of enactments. *Psychoanalytic Dialogues, 13*, 677–87.

Chused, J., Ellman, S., Renik, O., & Rothstein, A. (1999). Four aspects of the enactment concept: Definitions, therapeutic effects, dangers, history. *Journal of Clinical Psychoanalysis, 8*, 9–61.

Clyman, R. B. (1991). The procedural organization of emotions: A contribution from cognitive science to the psychoanalytic theory of therapeutic action. *Journal of the American Psychoanalytic Association, 39S*, 349–82.

Crittenden, P. (1999–2001). Attachment in adulthood: Coding manual for the dynamic-maturational approach to the adult attachment interview. Unpublished manuscript.

Davies, J. M. (1998). Multiple perspectives on multiplicity. *Psychoanalytic Dialogues, 8*, 195–206.

Davies, J. M. & Frawley, M. G. (1994). *Treating the Adult Survivor of Childhood Sexual Abuse: A Psychoanalytic Perspective.* New York: Basic Books.

Deutsch, H. (1937). Absence of grief. *Psychoanalytic Quarterly, 6,* 12–22.

Doehrman, M. (1976). Parallel processes in supervision and psychotherapy. *Bulletin of the Menninger Clinic, 40,* 3–104.

Dowling, S. (1982). Dreams and dreaming in relation to trauma in childhood. *International Journal of Psychoanalysis, 63,* 157–66.

Downey, T. W. (1994). Hans W. Loewald, M.D. (1906–93). *International Journal of Psychoanalysis, 75,* 839–42.

Druck, A. B. (1989). *Four Therapeutic Approaches to the Borderline Patient.* Northvale, NJ: Jason Aronson.

—— (2011). Modern structural theory. In A. B. Druck, C. Ellman, N. Freedman, & A. Thaler (Eds.), *A New Freudian Synthesis: Clinical Process in the Next Generation* (pp. 25–50). London: Karnac Books.

Dunn, J. (1995). Intersubjectivity in psychoanalysis: A critical review. *International Journal of Psychoanalysis, 76,* 723–38.

Eagle, M. & Wolitzky, D. (1986). Book review: *The process of psychoanalytic therapy: Models and strategies,* by E. Peterfreund. *Psychoanalysis and Contemporary Thought, 9,* 79–102.

Ekstein, R. (1965). A general treatment philosophy concerning acting out. In L. Abt & S. Weissman (Eds.), *Acting Out: Theoretical and Clinical Aspects* (pp. 162–72). New York: Grune & Stratton.

Ekstein, R. & Wallerstein, R. (1958). *The Teaching and Learning of Psychotherapy.* New York: Basic Books.

Ellman, C. (2011). Anonymity: Blank screen or black hole. In A. B. Druck, C. Ellman, N. Freedman, & A. Thaler (Eds.), *A New Freudian Synthesis: Clinical Process in the Next Generation* (pp. 157–72). London: Karnac Books.

Ellman, S. J. (1998). Enactment, transference, and analytic trust. In S. J. Ellman & M. Moskowitz (Eds.), *Enactment: Towards a New Approach in the Therapeutic Relationship* (pp. 183–205). Northvale, NJ: Jason Aronson.

—— (2007). Analytic trust and transference: Love, healing ruptures and facilitating repairs. *Psychoanalytic Inquiry, 27,* 246–63.

—— (2010). *When Theories Touch: A Historical and Theoretical Integration of Psychoanalytic Thought.* London: Karnac Books.

Erdelyi, M. (1974). A new look at the new look: Perceptual defense and vigilance. *Psychological Review, 81,* 1–25.

Ferenczi, S. (1932). *The Clinical Diary of Sandor Ferenczi* (ed. J. Dupont). Cambridge, MA: Harvard University Press (1988).

—— (1933). Confusion of tongues between adults and the child. In *Final Contributions to the Problems and Methods of Psychoanalysis* (pp. 156–67). London: Hogarth Press (1955).

Fleming, J. & Altschul, S. (1963). Activation of mourning and growth by psychoanalysis. *International Journal of Psychoanalysis, 44,* 419–31.

Fonagy, P. & Target, M. (1997). Perspectives on the recovered memories debate. In J. Sandler & P. Fonagy (Eds.), *Recovered Memories of Abuse: True or False?* (pp. 183–216). London: Karnac Books.

Frankel, J. (Chair) (2007). *Perspectives on Dissociation*. Panel presented at a January meeting of the Investigative Section of the Institute for Psychoanalytic Training and Research (IPTAR), New York, NY.

Frankiel, R. (1993). Hide-and-seek in the playroom: On object loss and transference in child treatment. *Psychoanalytic Review, 80*, 340–59.

Freedman, N. (1994). More on transformation: Enactments in psychoanalytic space. In A. D. Richards & A. K. Richards (Eds.), *The Spectrum of Psychoanalysis: Essays in Honor of Martin Bergmann* (pp. 93–110). Madison, CT: International Universities Press.

Freud, A. (1958). Adolescence. *Psychoanalytic Study of the Child, 13*, 255–78.

—— (1967). About losing and being lost. *Psychoanalytic Study of the Child, 22*, 9–19.

Freud, S. (1893–95). Studies on hysteria. In *The Standard Edition of the Complete Psychological Works of Sigmund Freud*, 24 vols. (ed. James Strachey). London: Hogarth Press (1956–1974), vol. II.

—— (1905). Fragment of an analysis of a case of hysteria. In *The Standard Edition of the Complete Psychological Works of Sigmund Freud*, 24 vols. (ed. James Strachey) (vol. VII, pp. 7–122). London: Hogarth Press (1956–1974).

—— (1910). Future prospects for psycho-analytic therapy. In *The Standard Edition of the Complete Psychological Works of Sigmund Freud*, 24 vols. (ed. James Strachey) (vol. XI, pp. 139–52). London: Hogarth Press (1956–1974).

—— (1912a). The dynamics of transference. In *The Standard Edition of the Complete Psychological Works of Sigmund Freud*, 24 vols. (ed. James Strachey) (vol. XII, pp. 97–108). London: Hogarth Press (1956–1974).

—— (1912b). Recommendations to physicians practising psycho-analysis. In *The Standard Edition of the Complete Psychological Works of Sigmund Freud*, 24 vols. (ed. James Strachey) (vol. XII, pp. 111–20). London: Hogarth Press (1956–1974).

—— (1914). Remembering, repeating and working-through. In *The Standard Edition of the Complete Psychological Works of Sigmund Freud*, 24 vols. (ed. James Strachey) (vol. XII, pp. 147–56). London: Hogarth Press (1956–1974).

—— (1915a). Observations on transference love. In *The Standard Edition of the Complete Psychological Works of Sigmund Freud*, 24 vols. (ed. James Strachey) (vol. XII, pp. 157–75). London: Hogarth Press (1956–1974).

—— (1915b). The unconscious. In *The Standard Edition of the Complete Psychological Works of Sigmund Freud*, 24 vols. (ed. James Strachey) (vol. XIV, pp. 159–216). London: Hogarth Press (1956–1974).

—— (1917). *Mourning and melancholia*. In *The Standard Edition of the Complete Psychological Works of Sigmund Freud*, 24 vols. (ed. James Strachey) (vol. XIV, pp. 237–58). London: Hogarth Press (1956–1974).

—— (1920). Beyond the pleasure principle. In *The Standard Edition of the Complete Psychological Works of Sigmund Freud*, 24 vols. (ed. James Strachey) (vol. XVIII, pp. 1–64). London: Hogarth Press (1956–1974).

—— (1923). The ego and the id. In *The Standard Edition of the Complete Psychological Works of Sigmund Freud*, 24 vols. (ed. James Strachey) (vol. XIX, pp. 12–68). London: Hogarth Press (1956–1974).

REFERENCES

—— (1927). Fetishism. In *The Standard Edition of the Complete Psychological Works of Sigmund Freud*, 24 vols. (ed. James Strachey) (vol. XXI, pp. 147–57). London: Hogarth Press (1956–1974).

—— (1940a). An outline of psycho-analysis. In *The Standard Edition of the Complete Psychological Works of Sigmund Freud*, 24 vols. (ed. James Strachey) (vol. XXIII, pp. 141–208). London: Hogarth Press (1956–1974).

—— (1940b). The splitting of the ego in the process of defense. In *The Standard Edition of the Complete Psychological Works of Sigmund Freud*, 24 vols. (ed. James Strachey) (vol. XXIII, pp. 271–78). London: Hogarth Press (1956–1974).

Gabbard, G. O. (1995). Countertransference: The emerging common ground. *International Journal of Psychoanalysis, 76*, 475–85.

Gediman, H. & Wolkenfeld, F. (1980). The parallelism phenomenon in psychoanalysis and supervision. Its reconsideration as a triadic system. *Psychoanalytic Quarterly, 49*, 234–55.

Gerson, S. (1996). Neutrality, resistance, and self-disclosure in an intersubjective psychoanalysis. *Psychoanalytic Dialogues, 6*, 623–45.

Greenberg, J. (2001). The analyst's participation: A new look. *Journal of the American Psychoanalytic Association, 49*, 359–81.

Gullestad, S. E. (2004). Who is "who" in dissociation? A plea for psychodynamics in a time of trauma. Paper presented at the *Joseph Sandler Conference on Dissociation*, March New Orleans, LA.

—— (2005). Who is "who" in dissociation? A plea for psychodynamics in a time of trauma. *International Journal of Psychoanalysis, 86*, 639–56.

Hanly, C. (1999). On subjectivity and objectivity in psychoanalysis. *Journal of the American Psychoanalytic Association, 47*, 427–44.

Harris, A. (2011). The relational tradition: Landscape and canon. *Journal of the American Psychoanalytic Association, 59*, 701–35.

Hartmann, H. (1964). On rational and irrational action. In *Essays on Ego Psychology* (pp. 37–68). New York: International Universities Press.

Heimann, P. (1950). On counter-transference. *International Journal of Psycho-Analysis, 31*, 81–84.

Hirsch, I. (1998). The concept of enactment and theoretical convergence. *Psychoanalytic Quarterly, 67*, 78–101.

Hoffman, I. Z. (1991). Discussion: Toward a social-constructivist view of the psychoanalytic situation. *Psychoanalytic Dialogues, 1*, 74–105.

—— (1992). Some practical implications of a social-constructivist view of the psychoanalytic situation. *Psychoanalytic Dialogues, 2*, 287–304.

Hurst, D. (1995). Panel report: Toward a definition of the term and concept of interaction. *Journal of the American Psychoanalytic Association, 43*, 517–37.

Hurvich, M. S. (1989). Traumatic moment, basic dangers and annihilation anxiety. *Psychoanalytic Psychology, 6*, 309–23.

—— (2004). Psychic trauma and fears of annihilation. In D. Knafo (Ed.), *Living with Terror, Working with Trauma: A Clinician's Handbook* (pp. 51–66). Northvale, NJ: Jason Aronson.

Ivey, G. (2008). Enactment controversies: A critical review of current debates. *International Journal of Psychoanalysis, 89*, 19–38.

Jacobs, T. (1986). Countertransference enactments. *Journal of the American Psychoanalytic Association, 34*, 289–307.

—— (1991). The interplay of enactments: Their role in the analytic process. In *The Use of the Self: Countertransference and Communication in the Analytic Situation* (pp. 31–49). Madison, CT: International Universities Press.

—— (1993). Insight and experience: Commentary on Morris Eagle's "Enactment, transference, and symptomatic cure." *Psychoanalytic Dialogues, 3*, 123–27.

—— (1994). Nonverbal communications. *Journal of the American Psychoanalytic Association, 42*, 741–62.

—— (1997). In search of the mind of the analyst: A progress report. *Journal of the American Psychoanalytic Association, 46*, 1129–67.

—— (2001a). On misreading and misleading patients: Some reflections on communications, miscommunications and countertransference enactments. *International Journal of Psychoanalysis, 82*, 653–69.

—— (2001b). On unconscious communications and covert enactments: Some reflections on their role in the analytic situation. *Psychoanalytic Inquiry, 21*, 4–23.

Jacobson, E. (1961). Adolescent moods and the remodeling of psychic structures in adolescence. *Psychoanalytic Study of the Child, 16*, 164–83.

—— (1964). *The Self and the Object World*. New York: International Universities Press.

Janet, P. (1889). *L'automatisme Psychologique*. Paris: Félix Alcan.

Johan, M. (1992). Panel report: Enactments in psychoanalysis. *Journal of the American Psychoanalytic Association, 40*, 827–41.

Joseph, B. (1989). *Psychic Equilibrium and Psychic Change: Selected Papers of Betty Joseph* (ed. M. Feldman & E. B. Spillius), London and New York: Routledge.

Kanzer, M. (1966). The motor sphere of the transference. *Psychoanalytic Quarterly, 35*, 522–39.

Katz, G. (1993). A death in the countertransference: A patient's unconscious enactment of object loss in the analytic relationship. Presented to the Division of Psychoanalysis (39), American Psychological Association, New York, NY.

—— (1995). Discussion of Dale Boesky's *Parallel Process and Supervision*. Presented at the Institute for Psychoanalytic Training and Research (IPTAR), March, New York, NY.

—— (1998). Where the action is: The enacted dimension of analytic process. *Journal of the American Psychoanalytic Association, 46*, 1129–67.

—— (2002). Missing in action: The enacted dimension of analytic process in a patient with traumatic object loss. In R. Lasky (Ed.), *Symbolization and Desymbolization: Essays in Honor of Norbert Freedman* (pp. 407–30). New York: Other Press.

—— (2011). Trauma in action: The enacted dimension of analytic process in a third generation Holocaust survivor. Discussion of "Secretly attached, secretly separate." In A. B. Druck, C. Ellman, N. Freedman, & A. Thaler (Eds.), *A New Freudian Synthesis: Clinical Process in the Next Generation* (pp. 239–47). London: Karnac Books.

Kern, J. (1987). Transference neurosis as a waking dream: Notes on a clinical enigma. *Journal of the American Psychoanalytic Association, 35*, 337–66.

Kernberg, O. (1965). Notes on countertransference. *Journal of the American Psychoanalytic Association, 13,* 38–56.

Killingmo, B. (1995). Affirmation in psychoanalysis. *International Journal of Psychoanalysis, 76,* 503–18.

—— (2006). A plea for affirmation: Relating to states of unmentalised affects. *Scandinavian Psychoanalytic Review, 29,* 13–21.

Klein, M. (1946). Notes on some schizoid mechanisms. *International Journal of Psychoanalysis, 27,* 99–110.

Lampl-De Groot, J. (1960). On adolescence. *Psychoanalytic Study of the Child, 15,* 95–103.

Laplanche, J. & Pontalis, J. B. (1967). *The Language of Psycho-Analysis* (trans. D. Nicholson Smith). New York: Norton Press (1973).

Lasky, R. (1993). Countertransference and the analytic instrument. In *Dynamics of Development and the Therapeutic Process* (pp. 263–96). Northvale, NJ: Jason Aronson.

Laub, D. & Auerhahn, N. C. (1989). Failed empathy: a central theme in the survivor's Holocaust experience. *Psychoanalytic Psychology, 6,* 377–400.

—— (1993). Knowing and not knowing massive psychic trauma: Forms of traumatic memory. *International Journal of Psychoanalysis, 74,* 287–302.

Laufer, M. (1966). Object loss and mourning during adolescence. *Psychoanalytic Study of the Child, 21,* 269–93.

Lennon, J. (1980). "Beautiful boy (darling boy)." *Double Fantasy.* Gefen Records.

Levenson, E. A. (1972). *The Fallacy of Understanding: An Inquiry into the Changing Structure of Psychoanalysis.* New York: Basic Books.

—— (1983). *The Ambiguity of Change: An Inquiry into the Nature of Psychoanalytic Reality.* New York: Basic Books.

—— (1988). Show and tell: The recursive order of transference. In A. Rothstein (Ed.), *How Does Treatment Help?* (pp. 135–43). Madison, CT: International Universities Press.

—— (2006). Response to John Steiner. *International Journal of Psychoanalysis, 87,* 321–24.

Loewald, H. (1960). On the therapeutic action of psychoanalysis. *International Journal of Psychoanalysis, 41,* 16–33.

—— (1970). Psychoanalytic theory and the psychoanalytic process. *Psychoanalytic Study of the Child, 25,* 45–68.

—— (1971). Some considerations on repetition and repetition compulsion. *International Journal of Psychoanalysis, 52,* 59–66.

—— (1975). Psychoanalysis as an art and the fantasy character of the psychoanalytic situation. *Journal of the American Psychoanalytic Association, 23,* 277–99.

—— (1976). Perspectives on memory. In *Papers on Psychoanalysis* (pp. 148–73). New Haven, CT: Yale University Press (1980).

—— (1979). Reflections on the psychoanalytic process and its therapeutic potential. *Psychoanalytic Study of the Child, 34,* 155–67.

—— (1986). Transference–countertransference. *Journal of the American Psychoanalytic Association, 34,* 275–87.

Louw, F. & Michael, P. (2001). Irreducible subjectivity and interactionism: A critique. *International Journal of Psychoanalysis, 82,* 747–65.

Lyons-Ruth, K. (1999). The two-person unconscious: Intersubjective dialogue, enactive relational representation, and the emergence of new forms of relational organization. *Psychoanalytic Inquiry, 19*, 576–617.

Main, M. & Goldwyn, R. (1998). Adult attachment scoring and classification system. Unpublished scoring manual, Department of Psychology, University of California, Berkeley, CA.

Maroda, K. J. (1998). Enactment: When the patient's and analyst's pasts converge. *Psychoanalytic Psychology, 15*, 517–35.

McLaughlin, J. (1987). The play of transference: Some reflections on enactment in the psychoanalytic situation. *Journal of the American Psychoanalytic Association, 35*, 557–82.

—— (1991). Clinical and theoretical aspects of enactment. *Journal of the American Psychoanalytic Association, 39*, 595–614.

Mitchell, S. (1988). *Relational Concepts in Psychoanalysis.* Cambridge, MA: Harvard University Press.

Nemiah, J. C. (1998). Early concepts of trauma, dissociation, and the unconscious: Their history and current implications. In J. D. Bremner & C. R. Marmar (Eds.), *Trauma, Memory, and Dissociation* (pp. 1–26). Washington, DC: American Psychiatric Press.

Oberman, N. C. (1990). Supervision and the achievement of an analytic identity. In R. C. Lane (Ed.), *Psychoanalytic Approaches to Supervision* (pp. 194–206). New York: Brunner/Mazel.

Ogden, T. (1994a). The analytic third: working with intersubjective clinical facts. *International Journal of Psychoanalysis, 75*, 3–20.

—— (1994b). *Subjects of Analysis.* Northvale, NJ: Jason Aronson.

—— (1996). Reconsidering three aspects of psychoanalytic technique. *International Journal of Psychoanalysis, 77*, 883–99.

Opatow, B. (1996). Panel report: Meaning in the clinical moment. *Journal of the American Psychoanalytic Association, 44*, 639–48.

Pegeron, J. P. (1996). Supervision as an analytic experience. *Psychoanalytic Quarterly, 65*, 693–710.

Poland, W. S. (1988). Insight and the analytic dyad. *Psychoanalytic Quarterly, 57*, 341–69.

—— (1992a). From analytic surface to analytic space. *Journal of the American Psychoanalytic Association, 40*, 381–404.

—— (1992b). Transference: "An original creation." *Psychoanalytic Quarterly, 61*, 185–205.

Racker, H. (1957). The meanings and uses of countertransference. *Psychoanalytic Quarterly, 26*, 303–57.

Rangell, L. (1989). Action theory within the structural view. *International Journal of Psychoanalysis, 70*, 189–203.

Reich, A. (1960). Further remarks on countertransference. *International Journal of Psychoanalysis, 41*, 389–95.

Reis, B. (2009). Performative and enactive features of psychoanalytic witnessing: The transference as the scene of address. *International Journal of Psychoanalysis, 90*, 1359–72.

Renik, O. (1993a). Countertransference enactment and the psychoanalytic process. In M. J. Horowitz, O. F. Kernberg, & E. M. Weinshel (Eds.), *Psychic Structure and Psychic Change: Essays in Honor of Robert S. Wallerstein, M.D.* (pp. 135–58). Madison, CT: International Universities Press.

—— (1993b). Analytic interaction: Conceptualizing technique in light of the analyst's irreducible subjectivity. *Psychoanalytic Quarterly, 62,* 553–71.

—— (1999). Playing one's cards face up in analysis: An approach to the problem of self-disclosure. *Psychoanalytic Quarterly, 68,* 521–39.

—— (2007). Intersubjectivity, therapeutic action, and analytic technique. *Psychoanalytic Quarterly, 76S,* 1547–62.

Roughton, R. E. (1993). Useful aspects of acting out: Repetition, enactment, and actualization. *Journal of the American Psychoanalytic Association, 41,* 443–72.

—— (1996). Action and acting out. In B. E. Moore (Ed.), *Psychoanalysis: The Major Concepts.* New Haven, CT: Yale University Press.

—— (1994). Repetition and interaction in the analytic process: Enactment, acting out, and collusion. *Annual of Psychoanalysis, 22,* 271–76.

Sachs, D. & Shapiro, S. (1976). On parallel processes in therapy and teaching. *Psychoanalytic Quarterly, 45,* 394–415.

Sandler, J. (1976). Countertransference and role-responsiveness. *International Review of Psycho-Analysis, 3,* 43–47.

—— (1993). On communication from patient to analyst: Not everything is projective identification. *International Journal of Psychoanalysis, 74,* 1097–107.

Sandler, J. & Sandler, A. M. (1997). A psychoanalytic theory of repression and the unconscious. In J. Sandler, & P. Fonagy (Eds.), *Recovered Memories of Abuse: True or False?* (pp. 163–81). London: Karnac Books.

Schafer, R. (1983). *The Analytic Attitude.* New York: Basic Books.

—— (1997). *The Contemporary Kleinians of London.* Madison, CT: International Universities Press.

Searles, H. (1955). The informational value of the supervisor's emotional experiences. *Psychiatry, 18,* 135–46.

Segel, N. (1969). Repetition compulsion, acting out, and identification with the doer. *Journal of the American Psychoanalytic Association, 17,* 474–88.

Sinason, V. (2002). The shoemaker and the elves: working with multiplicity. In V. Sinason (Ed.), *Attachment, Trauma and Multiplicity: Working with Dissociative Identity Disorder* (pp. 125–38). Hove: Brunner-Routledge.

Singer, J. A. & Conway, M. A. (2011). Reconsidering therapeutic action: Loewald, cognitive neuroscience and the integration of memory's duality. *International Journal of Psychoanalysis, 92,* 1183–207.

Smith, H. F. (1993a). Engagements in the analytic work. *Psychoanalytic Inquiry, 13,* 425–54.

—— (1993b). The analytic surface and the discovery of enactment. *Annual of Psychoanalysis, 21,* 243–55.

—— (1997). Resistance, enactment, and interpretation: A self-analytic study. *Psychoanalytic Inquiry, 17,* 13–30.

REFERENCES

—— (2000). Countertransference, conflictual listening, and the analytic object relationship. *Journal of the American Psychoanalytic Association, 48*, 95–128.

Spillius, E. B. (1992). Clinical experiences of projective identification. In R. Anderson (Ed.), *Clinical Lectures on Klein and Bion* (pp. 59–73). London: Tavistock/Routledge.

Steiner, J. (2006). Interpretative enactments and the analytic setting. *International Journal of Psychoanalysis, 87*, 315–20.

Steingart, I. (1995). *A Thing Apart: Love and Reality in the Therapeutic Relationship.* Northvale, NJ: Jason Aronson.

—— (2009). Microwaves, fields, and clinical process. Paper presented as part of the panel: *Radical Integrations in Psychoanalytic Technique*, Institute for Psychoanalytic Training and Research (IPTAR), December, New York, NY.

Stern, D. B. (2009). *Partners In Thought: Working with Unformulated Experience, Dissociation, and Enactment.* New York, NY: Routledge.

Stern, D. N. (1985). *The Interpersonal World of the Infant.* New York: Basic Books.

Stolorow, R. D. & Atwood, G. E. (1992). *Contexts of Being.* Hillsdale, NJ: Analytic Press.

Stolorow, R. D., Atwood, G. E., & Ross, J. M. (1978). The representational world in psychoanalytic therapy. *International Review of Psycho-Analysis, 5*, 247–56.

Talby-Abarbanel, M. (2011). Secretly attached, secretly separate: Art, dreams, and transference–countertransference in the analysis of a third generation Holocaust survivor. In A. B. Druck, C. Ellman, N. Freedman, & A. Thaler, *A new Freudian Synthesis: Clinical Process in the Next Generation* (pp. 219–37). London: Karnac Books.

Teicholz, J. G. (1990). *Kohut, Loewald, and the Postmoderns: A Comparative Study of Self and Relationship.* Hillsdale, NJ: The Analytic Press.

Tower, L. E. (1956). Countertransference. *Journal of the American Psychoanalytic Association, 4*, 224–55.

Vivona, J. M. (2003). Embracing figures of speech: The transformative potential of spoken language. *Psychoanalytic Psychology, 20*, 52–66.

—— (2006). From developmental metaphor to developmental model: The shrinking role of language in the talking cure. *Journal of the American Psychoanalytic Association, 54*, 877–902.

—— (2009a). Leaping from brain to mind: A critique of mirror neuron explanations of countertransference. *Journal of the American Psychoanalytic Association, 57*, 525–50.

—— (2009b). Embodied language in neuroscience and psychoanalysis. *Journal of the American Psychoanalytic Association, 57*, 1327–60.

Winnicott, D. W. (1963). Dependence in infant-care, in child-care, and in the psycho-analytical setting. In *The Maturational Process and the Facilitating Environment* (pp. 249–59). London: Hogarth Press (1965).

Wolfenstein, M. (1966). How is mourning possible? *Psychoanalytic Study of the Child, 21*, 93–123.

—— (1969). Loss, rage, and repetition. *Psychoanalytic Study of the Child, 24*, 432–60.

INDEX